Girl, I Love That Dress! And Your Eye Shadow!

Learning Acceptance, the Girl Way

Echo Miller

Table of Contents

Introduction

Hey there, gorgeous! Let me tell you a story. Back when I was 15 years old, there was this girl named Anna, who was the prettiest, most gorgeous, and smartest person that everyone admired. She was the prom queen, the topper of the class, and even the class president. She appeared confident, sassy, and was popular. Everybody at the high school wanted to be friends with Anna. Of course, I did too!

Do you want to know how Anna also had moments that tarnished her confidence and self-esteem? She is going to narrate her story from the annual function to you girls! I am sure you can relate to it, so let's listen to her.

My story is from a few years back when I participated in my school's annual talent show. I have this memory in my mind so clearly, just like it happened yesterday. You will soon know why it's so clear in my head up till now!

I have been working on my dance routine for several weeks and was looking forward to demonstrating my abilities on stage. When I got on the stage, I was quite anxious, but I knew I would rock it if I stayed confident. Within two minutes, literally two, I heard a sudden rip sound coming from the back of my pants.

When I realized that my pants had ripped open, exposing a substantial portion of my underwear to the entire audience, my heart started sinking.

At that time, I felt a surge of humiliation and reluctance. In the crowd, I could see the shocked and amused expressions on the faces of my classmates, teachers, and even my crush. OMG, How embarrassing, No? I wanted to vanish and run so far away!

I closed my eyes for a second to regain my composure and started giving myself positive self-statements like,

Anna, you can deal with it for sure!

You know it's only a moment you are going to manage it.

You are strong and resilient, and your energy is unmatched. You can definitely get over this!

I reminded myself that I can choose how I respond to this circumstance. I took a deep breath and transformed my humiliation into a chance for laughing and self-acknowledgment.

I acknowledged the mishap. I knew this had happened, so I had to deal with it with sanity. I looked at the audience with a grin on my face. I said something along the lines of, "Well, it seems like my pants wanted to join the show too," in a lighthearted joke about the unanticipated wardrobe malfunction. The crowd laughed uncontrollably, and my confidence re-emerged. That moment was crazy indeed, but to be honest, it made me feel way more confident!

I continued dancing excitedly, moving my heart out regardless of the wardrobe malfunction. I demonstrated resilience and the ability to laugh at myself by accepting the situation. You will also agree that I did not see that coming so, what's the point of feeling under-confident? Right?

After the astounding performance, I got an overflow of help from my companions, instructors, and even outsiders, who were dazzled by my capacity to deal with a humiliating circumstance with effortlessness and a funny tone. Their support meant the world to me, and it still helps me do wonders in my life! That day I realized that my embarrassment does not define me; rather, it is a normal part of life.

So, girls, hope you got to learn something from Anna's experience. This experience shows Anna and all the young ladies that humiliating moments happen to everybody. What really matters is how we respond to those times. We can develop resilience, self-acceptance, and the confidence to deal with similar situations in the future by having the courage to laugh at ourselves and not take ourselves too seriously.

Despite being the diva that Anna still is, she felt ashamed and embarrassed. But her reaction made her stand out in the crowd proving that she is the queen! Yet that day, I realized how hard it must be for my friend to maintain her social image. It must be tough for her to try to meet everybody's expectations.

If a prom queen can have such problems that affect her self-esteem, why do you think you are alone in this? Chin up, sweetheart.

It's time to buckle up because I'm about to take your teenage years to the next level. I'll hold your hand, guide you through the challenges, and share the secret strategies to win in this journey.

Now picture this: You walk into a room, rocking in that stunning dress that feels like a million bucks. Your eye-catching flawless eye makeup and lipstick compliment your look, making the heads turn, and jaws drop. You're confidently taking every step with your favorite high heels. And then—the compliments begin to pour in, just like a summer rainstorm.

I read somewhere...

> *Justin: "Girls like compliments, don't they?"*

> *Madeline: "I think everyone does if it's sincere. Not just girls."*

—Katie Kacvinsky, Awaken

Okay, now pause for a moment and think how important compliments are and how they make anyone feel so powerful. They hold an incredible ability to brighten up our day, lift our confidence, and strengthen our connection with those around us. But do you know what the secret sauce is? It's not just the compliments themselves but the choices you make, the fashion you embrace, and the artistry you apply to your face. That's what opens up the world of self-expression.

Hold up, sister! I know what you must be thinking right now. The path to self-expression isn't always smooth sailing. Societal pressure, self-doubt, and insecurities; that's all teenage years come with.

The struggle is real, and I completely feel you. That's why I'm here. I will discuss all of the problems and pain you're experiencing right now. Because, you know, I've been through this all. I know what it takes to level up your confidence during times when you feel the lowest about yourself.

Now tell me, what bothers you? Is it that nagging feeling that you're constantly worrying about what people think of you? Or the struggle to find the perfect outfit that just fits right? Maybe, it's the pressure to mold you according to so-called societal standards? And let's not forget about the never-ending race on social media that makes you question your worth.

But you. You, my gorgeous lady, don't have to worry anymore. This book is your motivation to change for the better. It's here to lift you, guide you through the maze of teenage life, and empower you to embrace your authentic self with style, grace, and a touch of sass.

So, are you ready to start this journey? If so, hold on tight, as it is packed with lots of shortcuts, insider tips, and life-alerting wisdom. Here you'll learn all the secrets to conquering your fears, building up unshakable self-confidence, and forming meaningful relationships with others.

With interactive activities and relatable stories, you'll have everything you need to handle the twists and turns of your teenage era like a pro.

Oh, and wait. I almost forgot to mention the extreme testimonials! They are seriously so amazing. I have those too! Have you seen all the celebs who have totally strutted down the red carpet of life with so much confidence showing off their own unique styles and just radiating major girl power vibes? Their stories are inspiring enough to remind you that you're not alone on this journey for sure.

Now, let me paint a vivid picture of the amazing outcome that's just waiting for you on the other side.

Imagine a life where you jump out of bed every morning, eager to show the world your true colors, free from the pressure of what other people might think. It's beautiful, right?

Imagine yourself confidently acing every task, ready to take on new adventures, and making choices that truly make you happy.

Relationships? Oh, they'll definitely be healthier. You'll be surrounded by people who truly appreciate and value you for who you are. Also, you'll feel healthier and happier than ever before.

And what makes me the right person to lead you on this journey? The same experience. Yes, I've been where you are right now. I have overcome obstacles, danced with my insecurities, and come out on the other side stronger, wiser, and with a killer wardrobe. I have discovered these secrets through years of self-development, research, and embracing my own girl power. Trust me; I can't wait to spill the beans to you.

Back in the day, before my transformation phase, it wasn't easy at all. We didn't have the support and strategies we needed then. Sometimes, I can't believe how far I've come. But you, my beautiful, have the support that you need to win the world. Times have changed, and so will you!

So, here's the deal: you've found the perfect book. It's a wealth of advice seasoned with wit, tales, and that appealing Valley Girl charm. You will laugh, you will learn, and you will find your inner unconquerable girl power.

Let's take fashion as our shield, our ability to express ourselves as our weapon, and charge headlong into this adventure together. It's time to walk confidently in your wonderful shoes, glow bright like the star that you are, and take over the world.

Are you ready? Come on, let's do this!

Chapter 1:

Embracing Your Authentic Self

You are more powerful than you know; you are beautiful just as you are. –Melissa Etheridge

The time has come to truly embrace yourself, my girl. Welcome to the first section of our journey of positive growth together. This chapter will dig into the extraordinary way of embracing your authentic self. Prepare to open the unmatched power that exists in you as we investigate the excellence of figuring out your uniqueness, embracing your flaws, and cultivating self-acknowledgment.

We will plunge into the extraordinary force of perceiving and commending your strengths, interests, and abilities. We will investigate how accepting your individuality can bring joy, fulfillment, and a sense of direction to your life.

Every single one of us is like a wonderful mosaic, made out of interesting pieces that make us what our identity is. We must acknowledge that our unique combination of talents, interests, and strengths distinguishes us from others.

Living in a world where everyone shares the same talents, interests, and personalities wouldn't be very interesting. Would it? The diversity, color, and vibrancy of our differences enrich the fabric of life.

Thus, if you feel less confident about your looks, know that you are unique, and uniqueness is pretty. You need to own what you truly are. With that, let me help you understand your uniqueness and accept it by heart in this chapter. Read on.

Understanding Your Uniqueness

You, my beautiful woman, are a masterpiece unlike any other. A unique combination of qualities, abilities, and strengths within you is just waiting to be discovered and appreciated.

Reflect on what makes you stand out from the crowd and what makes you shine. It could be your ability to deeply empathize with others, your sense of humor, or your artistic talent. Embrace these characteristics, for they are the substance of your uniqueness.

Each young lady around you has a unique set of qualities, abilities, and strengths that make her unique. Your individuality is unmatched, just like a fingerprint. You can bring something unique to the world by accepting yourself as you are.

The following qualities distinguish you from your peers, making you understand that you are the main character of your story!

Genetics

It's time you unleash your uniqueness that is decided by your genetic makeup. Every genetic combination is gorgeous and helps you harness your power from deep within you.

The distinction of your genes makes you realize how unique you are from the very beginning of your existence.

Your individuality leads you to emphasize your unique inner self through your DNA that, despite being inherent in your parents, is one-of-a-kind. Look how beautifully nature gives you signs to prove that you are rare.

Personality

Have you ever wondered how we possess different traits that define our personality and its unique attributes? My love, we are the epitome of strength and beauty like no other. The core of who we actually are reflects in our personality. The individual combination of our thoughts, feelings, and actions is what makes us.

We interact with the world in our own unique patterns and ways. Some people might think of us as sociable and outgoing, while some might think of us as more reserved and reflective.

Since they enrich our relationships and interactions, we should embrace our personality traits of kindness, creativity, and determination. Being consistent with our character permits us to connect with others on a deeper level.

Intellect

Our minds are intriguing parts of what make us extraordinary. They envelop our ability to get the hang of things, critical thinking, and innovativeness. Individual preferences and intellectual strengths are unique to each of us.

On some days, we are great at thinking analytically, while on other days, we are drawn to our artistic or intuitive skills.

Our intellectual pursuits and interests shape our worldviews and approaches to challenges. We are able to discover our passions and make distinctive contributions when we embrace our intellectual individuality.

Goals

Our goals and objectives give us a feeling of direction and course throughout everyday life. They are a representation of our aspirations, desires, and self-concepts.

Our values, interests, and personal experiences form the foundation of our goals. Whether they include self-awareness, vocational accomplishments, connections, or having a constructive outcome on society, they provide us with a feeling of importance and inspiration.

Experiences

I, myself, have been profoundly shaped by my life experiences. Each of our journeys has had its own set of triumphs, challenges, relationships, and adventures. Our wisdom, resilience, empathy, and knowledge have grown due to these experiences.

They have given us remarkable points of view on the world, affecting our qualities, convictions, and ways of behaving. We gain a deeper comprehension of both ourselves and each other by accepting our positive and negative experiences. They support our personal development and cultivate empathy for others.

I want to tell you about Lily, my adorable young cousin. She was so beautiful and talented, yet she had so many insecurities about herself. She was passionate about dancing, but her fear of not being good enough always kept her from performing onstage. From an early age, she tracked down delight and opportunity in articulating her thoughts through dance moves. She signed up for dance lessons and practiced and honed her skills for a long time. Meanwhile, she frequently compared her skills with those of her fellow dancers. She would feel inadequate and doubt her own talent as she observed their graceful movements and intricate routines.

Lily once had the chance to compete in a national-level dance competition. It was quite an opportunity, to be honest! She realized she had a decision to make as she stood backstage, nerves coursing through her body. She could either let unrealistic comparisons and self-doubt consume her, or she could embrace her interesting style and sparkle with certainty.

At that time, Lily settled on a choice. She took a deep breath, closed her eyes, and imagined dancing like no one had ever seen her before. She recalled the excitement and passion she felt as she moved to the music's rhythm. Lily felt the spotlight on her as she stepped onto the stage, and she let her body tell the story in her heart.

You know what? She discovered something extraordinary as she danced! It had nothing to do with being the best dancer or copying other people's moves. It was about bringing her own interpretation to the art form and showcasing her distinctive style. She realized that her dance was truly unique because of her experiences, feelings, and personal expression. Isn't it an amazing thing to feel? Self-expression at its best, right? She praised other dancers but also learned that she also has unique moves to impress the world!

Lily has embraced her uniqueness wholeheartedly ever since that day. She, as of now, has not contrasted herself with others yet centered on praising her individuality. Her self-confidence and certainty developed, and she turned into a wellspring of motivation for her companions. Many people were moved by her ability to express herself through her dance and remind them that true beauty is embracing one's unique gifts.

Lily's experience is a powerful reminder that the experiences we have and how we choose to embrace them shape our individuality. Each of us has a unique perspective, abilities to share, and a story to tell. By recognizing and embracing our encounters, we can better comprehend our uniqueness and the worth we bring to the world. You must take steps to embrace your uniqueness.

It is essential to acknowledge our unique differences and celebrate them. Like puzzle pieces, our interests, abilities, and personalities fit together to form a singular picture. Lily's experience helps us figure out ways to explore our personality's uniqueness in the following ways:

Respect Yourself and Others

In my humble opinion, respect is the key to finding peace despite our differences. Embracing our individuality, living life, and, most importantly, letting life happen should be our priority.

Celebrate Others for Their Uniqueness

Celebrating the other person for who they are is another way to embrace our uniqueness—letting them shine their own light, knowing that they can. We are undeniably called to play our own roles in the world, but our motivation to love someone is something ultimately similar. Girl, fly high and respect the peculiarities of the other person. Because we all had different upbringings, even siblings who have lived together for a long time might end up being different people with different points of view. So, imagine how uniqueness is noticeable in everyone around us.

Listen to Your Heart

Pay attention to your heart, and stand firm. Be amped up for yourself and even acknowledge your oddness. It will take you somewhere magical if you do this. Nothing can stop you; take the chance. Anything is possible! Try not to fear being interesting because that is the main way you will become the best version of yourself.

Recognize Your Hidden Skills

In this section, we have explored how crucial it is to recognize our individual talents, interests, and strengths. By praising our disparities, we make space for self-acknowledgment and self-improvement.

Remember that each of us possesses a distinctive combination of characteristics that make the world beautiful. Celebrate what makes you

unique, pursue your passions, and embrace your strengths. Doing so will allow you to experience the incredible power and joy of fully accepting your individuality.

Embrace Your Own Uniqueness

To really embrace your uniqueness, it's fundamental to distinguish your extraordinary set of abilities. Accept the qualities and characteristics that set you apart, whether these qualities are your skills, interests, personal style, or anything. Just don't be afraid to be yourself. Praise your interests and let them sparkle, for they are an indispensable part of what your identity is.

Each of us possesses a unique energy force. There is no one in the universe like you. That ought to be celebrated rather than hidden. Comparison destroys your satisfaction and contentment. You combine everything that life has given you perfectly. Your encounters, great and awful, have formed you into your identity. And what's more? You can make use of those experiences and insights to your advantage.

Contrasting yourself with others and utilizing their background to shape your own will lessen your own self-esteem and will stop you from finding your real purpose throughout everyday life. Acknowledge that you are bound to follow your own way, paying little heed to what the world is doing. The options are endless!

Ask yourself, what do you need to accomplish? What have you accomplished as of now? How did your life lead you to various locations? What has changed about your body over time? Isn't everything about it what makes you unique?

Utilize skills that enable you to demonstrate your individuality to express yourself. Allow your creativity to flow onto the canvas if you are passionate about painting. Assuming that you love dancing, let your body move uninhibitedly to the beat of your heart. Assuming composing poems addresses your spirit, let your words paint striking pictures and inspire feelings.

Keep in mind that a person's opinion of you is nothing that you should be worried about.

Let me give you a personal example; I am sure you will learn a lot from it. When I was 16 years old, I had always had a strong interest in art and wanted to be a successful painter. I had a lot of fun and could express myself in ways that words couldn't by making beautiful art.

I once found the strength to exhibit my artwork at a regional art show. I couldn't help but overhear some whispers and comments from people passing by as I stood next to my paintings, eager to share my passion with the world.

"I have no idea what this is." Unaware of how much their words hurt me, one person chuckled and said, "It looks like a child's doodle."

"Who does she think she is, Pablo Picasso?" Another person made this comment, and their dismissive tone cut through my excitement.

Self-doubt began to creep in. I began scrutinizing my capacities and contemplating whether I was simply tricking myself by seeking after arts. I felt as though the opinions of those strangers were a heavy burden that threatened to crush my dreams.

But then, with a warm smile, a kind older woman approached me. "You know, art is subjective," she said after pondering my work for some time. The feelings your paintings evoke, the stories they tell, and the joy they bring to those who connect with them are what really matter. Try not to let the pessimistic assessments of a couple of individuals beat you down."

Her words touched my heart! Like honestly, I was in awe. I comprehended that everybody has various preferences and inclinations, and not every person will appreciate or grasp my creative vision—and that is totally OK.

I promised myself that I would put my own happiness first and continue my artistic journey without seeking approval from anyone from that point forward. I continued to create art that reflected my unique perspective and spoke to my soul.

My artwork began to gain recognition over time. Those who connected with my style and narrative began to appreciate my talent and artistic voice. My self-assurance increased with each brushstroke, and I learned to place my own opinion above all others.

This experience taught me a valuable lesson: The slippery slope of seeking validation from other people can stifle our true potential and hinder our personal development.

My fellow dreamers, remember that they have a novel voice and viewpoint that should be heard. Don't let those who doubt or disagree with you dim your vision. Keep coming up with new ideas, keep expressing yourself, and most importantly, keep having faith in yourself. Your journey is well worth it, and you can achieve your goals. Go out there, embrace your uniqueness, and let your specialty radiate brilliantly!

Embracing Imperfections

Do you usually question your worth when you make a mistake? Do you expect yourself to perform perfectly in every task? Do you set high standards for yourself and prevent doing things that make you happy just because you don't want people to think low of you? Don't do that. That's unhealthy and will always make you feel less of yourself and more of them.

- **You did not come to please the world:** My dear, know that you are not here to please the world; instead, you have to keep yourself content to make your life journey worthwhile! Your unique personality will nurture once you start accepting your flaws and shortcomings.

- **Perfection is overrated:** Let's talk about your flaws and quirks which make you perfectly imperfect. We will discuss the powerful idea that perfection is overrated and that our flaws are what make us unique as humans in this section. We'll talk about how beautiful it is to accept our mistakes, failures, and flaws as opportunities for development and self-discovery. Let's set out on this journey of self-acceptance and appreciate the beautiful mess that comes with being human!

- **Stop hiding your flaws:** Society may tell you that flaws should be hidden or fixed, but we're here to change the narrative. Accepting one's flaws is a superpower in and of itself. Recognizing everyone makes mistakes sometimes and tracking down magnificence in the crude, unfiltered parts of your being.

- **Comparison is unhealthy**: The issue isn't that we're flawed. The issue is we imagine that most people aren't. We think their lives are perfect or close to it. We naturally feel inadequate when we compare ourselves to other people. We believe: What's going on with me? Everyone else seems to have everything figured out. It would appear that no one else is having trouble.

However, even if all of these external indicators of a perfect life are accurate, they are only part of the story. They don't let you know that behind that apparently blissful marriage is a controlling life partner, and behind that thin body is an eating disorder, and the delightful children actually don't stay asleep for the entire night.

Think of when you strived to do everything right and aimed to achieve perfection in yourself. Maybe it was affected by parental assumptions or cultural tensions. But you know what? Being imperfect is adorable.

When I was 15 years old, I decided to audition for the school play. I had been putting my singing and acting skills to the test for months because it was a goal of mine to perform on stage. I was both excited and nervous as the day of the audition arrived.

My hands trembled, and my heart raced as I stepped onto the stage to sing my chosen song. I started to sing; however, part of the way through, I failed to remember the verses. I stumbled over my words as I was overcome with panic, embarrassed, and disappointed in myself.

I couldn't help but replay the audition in my head and scold myself for my mistakes. I was discouraged because I believed that my chances of getting a role had been eliminated. Nonetheless, something inside me moved.

I made the decision to accept my imperfections rather than dwelling on them. I came to the realization that my worth as a performer and my talent were not based on my ability to forget the lyrics. It was only a minor setback in a much longer journey.

With freshly discovered assurance, I moved toward the chief and communicated my certified energy for being a piece of the creation. I conveyed my enthusiasm for performing and readiness to improve. The director surprised me by admiring my authenticity and resilience despite my error.

I was given a supporting job in the play, and throughout the presentation process, I embraced each defect that came in my direction. During rehearsals, I stumbled over lines, missed a few cues, and occasionally even hit the wrong notes, but I never let those experiences define me.

I realized that creativity and development go hand in hand. It's what sets each performance apart and draws the audience in. I was able to fully enjoy the experience and develop a deeper connection with the audience by accepting my flaws.

That play taught me a valuable lesson in retrospect: Being flawless is not the goal. It's about embracing our beautiful imperfections and appreciating the journey of self-discovery and growth.

So, my dear friends, don't fear failing to achieve perfection or making mistakes. Embrace your characteristics, your incidents, and your exceptional approach to getting things done. In those flaws, you'll track down legitimacy and genuine excellence.

Embrace the flaws that make you human, for they are the venturing stones to self-revelation and self-improvement.

Make Vulnerability Your Strength

Accepting one's flaws implies accepting one's vulnerability. At the point when we permit ourselves to be defenseless, we make further associations with others. Take risks, express your feelings, and accept your vulnerabilities by embracing them. Vulnerability is the path to genuine connections and personal development, as it helps you create true relationships!

Imperfection Is Adorable

Your body is one of a kind; your skin's blemishes make you look beautiful. It's all a part of nature. We are bound to feel alive through our imperfections, for they help us identify and recognize how we conquer the battles of the world through our uniqueness.

So let go of the insecurities and look for opportunities for self-exploration. Start your journey toward self-acceptance and see how your life becomes your favorite fairy tale!

Learn the Hidden Lessons

Our flaws teach us valuable lessons and growth opportunities. They make us resilient and empathetic.

We tend to appreciate the beauty in accepting our flaws. We interface with each other on a more spiritual level through our interactions. Remember that perfection is not required; it's tied to being real. Let me give you a testimonial on how you can learn beautiful lessons and chances of personal growth from your flaws.

"Growing up, I generally felt compelled to be amazing in all that I did. I strived for extraordinary grades, a flawless appearance, and a truly amazing life. However, despite my best efforts, I could not meet those unreasonable expectations.

I didn't realize the hidden benefits of accepting my flaws until I was confronted with a significant setback in my life. I failed my 9th-grade final exam! My failure shattered my confidence, left me feeling helpless and defeated, and I had a choice at that point: to either let my flaws define me or use them to grow.

I decided to change my subject. I was studying science even though I was not slightly interested in it. I took up math as my major instead, and I noticed a positive change in my results. I began to see my blemishes as significant examples and potentially open doors for personal growth.

Embracing my flaws made me stronger and more compassionate. I figured out how to see the value in excellence and commend my extraordinary excursion. I found that being real and authentic is more important than striving for perfection.

I now wear my flaws as honor badges with pride. They help me to remember my solidarity, my versatility, and the important examples I've advanced along the way. I no longer have to worry about being judged or making mistakes. All things being equal, I embrace them as a component of my story and offer them to others to move and elevate.

Know that you are not alone if you feel weighed down by your flaws. Embrace your flaws, for they hold the ability to shape you into a more grounded, more merciful, and genuinely credible person. Keep in mind that perfection is not necessary; learn the hidden lessons from your experiences, and grow from them. It's about accepting yourself for who you are and appreciating the beautiful, imperfect journey that is life." —Emily, 16 years.

Accepting Yourself

Now, let's get started on the life-changing idea of self-acceptance. It involves accepting all aspects of oneself, including the positive, negative, and even the flawed. Self-acknowledgment is the foundation of exploring the difficulties of adolescence and fostering a solid mental self-image.

We will look at how challenging negative self-talk and societal pressures can have a significant impact. It has been seen that 58% of youngsters stress unnecessarily over what other people think of them. Self-depreciation and a lack of self-acceptance lead to chronic depression and high levels of anxiety. Many young people are self-conscious because of social and developmental factors.

It would help if you kept the given things in mind to improve self-acceptance:

- **Strategically Enhance Self-Acceptance:** I will strive to encourage self-acceptance so we embrace our true selves by providing practical strategies and exercises. From positive confirmations to caring for oneself, we will relinquish self-judgment and embrace our innate values. Let's begin the empowering process of cultivating self-acceptance and recognizing our unique beauty.

- **External Validation Is Not Necessary:** We are freed from the burden of constantly seeking external validation when we accept who we are. We recognize our value and the fact that we are sufficient in our current state. We gain the ability to live authentically and open the door to self-love through self-acceptance.

- **Surround Yourself With Optimistic Souls:** In our quest for self-acceptance, the people we surround ourselves with play a crucial role. I used to assess every one of my connections and groups of friends to understand what they meant for my excursion of development throughout everyday life.

Benefits of Self-Acceptance

My girl, you are unaware of how self-acceptance can benefit you in the long run. Your family, your peers, your relationships, and most importantly, you yourself will flourish in life.

We tend to focus on the positives, right? So, let's dive into comprehending the beneficial impact self-acceptance has on us.

Better Mental and Emotional Health

Acceptance of self encourages a positive mental self-image and develops self-empathy. We can improve our mental and emotional well-being by accepting ourselves as we are and cultivating a more positive relationship with ourselves.

It improves happiness, lowers anxiety, and reduces self-judgment. Self-acceptance is a necessary step toward self-improvement and essential to our mental and physical health.

Self-acknowledgment has been a unique advantage in my life, changing my mental prosperity in manners I never imagined. I struggled for a long time with constantly comparing myself to others, having the impression that I wasn't good enough, and looking for external validation to fill the void in me.

However, as I began a journey of self-acceptance and self-discovery, I became aware of its enormous power.

My emotional and mental health significantly improved as I fully accepted myself. I forgave myself for my perceived shortcomings and became more at peace with my previous mistakes. I felt a new sense of inner peace and contentment as the heavy burden of shame and guilt lifted. So, if you're on a similar journey, I encourage you to embrace your uniqueness, celebrate it, and set out on the life-changing path of self-acceptance. An excursion prompts better emotional wellness, preparing you for a genuinely satisfying life.

Strengthened Resilience

Adolescence is a time of change, growth, and overcoming new obstacles. Self-acknowledgment furnishes flexibility, empowering you to return quickly from difficulties, disappointments, and dismissals. It helps you develop a growth mindset and the ability to see difficulties as opportunities for learning and development.

Instilling Confidence

We all love a little glow of confidence on us, right? You can gain confidence and the ability to be true to your values and beliefs when you embrace yourself authentically. You are able to express your thoughts, opinions, and feelings without fear of being judged, which results in more meaningful and genuine connections with other people.

Lasting Relationships

At the point when young people acknowledge and adore themselves, it's easier to foster better associations with others. So, you are bound to define limits, impart actuality, and draw connections that align with your actual selves. How amazing is this! You get encouraged to surround yourself with positive, encouraging people who value and respect you when you cultivate self-acceptance.

Enhancing Decision-Making Ability

If you have a healthy sense of self-acceptance, you can make better choices that are in line with who you really are. You do not rely on external validation or conform to the demands of society. It helps you trust yourself and allows you to trust your gut, follow your values, and take responsibility for your actions. So, get ready to make your own decisions. The best ones!

Let's have a heart-to-heart conversation here, girls! I will quote the story of my dear companion that intrigues and motivates me to be more accepting of myself. As a youngster, she battled with low confidence and a consistent sensation of not being sufficient. Her insecurities were exacerbated by her being surrounded by friends who frequently engaged in negative self-talk and comparison.

She went to a self-improvement workshop once, where she met a group of people who exuded positivity and acceptance. They accepted her as she was and provided a secure and encouraging setting where she could freely express herself without fear of being judged. She consciously decided to surround herself with these positive influences after being inspired by their outlook on life.

She began to notice a significant shift in her outlook and well-being as she spent more time with her new friends. They encouraged one another to focus on their strengths and celebrate their accomplishments rather than having conversations that made them feel bad about themselves.

She felt empowered to express her passions and dreams without fear of ridicule or criticism. They encouraged her to embrace her individuality and celebrated her uniqueness. They showed her the worth of self-acknowledgment and the significance of taking care of oneself. Self-compassion and affirming beliefs gradually replaced her negative self-talk as she challenged it.

With their help, she bravely left on new undertakings and sought after her interests. She began writing, which she had always wanted to do but was too afraid to do. She was supported unwaveringly and constructively by her new circle of positive people who cheered her on.

Her story serves as a reminder that the people we surround ourselves with significantly impact how we perceive ourselves and how we grow as individuals. We can foster self-acceptance and the ability to live authentically by seeking out positive and accepting influences.

Promoting Self-Acceptance

Following are some ways you can make sure to promote self-acceptance:

- First and foremost, keep in mind that you are still a teenager in her learning phase. Accept that personal development is a journey that lasts a lifetime. Allow yourself to make errors and learn from them. Knowing that growth takes time and patience permits you to develop.

- Then, forgiveness is vital. Accept self-forgiveness for past errors or perceived shortcomings. Feeling guilty just obstructs your advancement. Let go of your self-criticism and embrace the power of forgiveness. Keep in mind that you are deserving of understanding and compassion.

- Practice self-empathy by treating yourself with thoughtfulness and understanding. Be kind to one another in your words and deeds. Indulge yourself as you would a dear companion, offering affection and support. Remind yourself that you are doing your best when difficulties arise, which is sufficient.

- Love yourself and acknowledge your strengths, abilities, and talents. Well, who owns the world? Certainly us! Regardless of how insignificant they may appear, be proud of your achievements. Know that your individual talents and gifts are a part of the vibrant fabric of your life, so take advantage of them.

- Quiet your inner critic, that voice of self-doubt and pessimism. Recognize that this negative voice in your head does not accurately represent who you are. Replace negative self-talk with positive affirmations to combat it. Encircle yourself with positive impacts and steady individuals who inspire and empower you. You are Unstoppable!

- Lastly, build up your inner circle—a group of people who love and accept you for who you are. Encircle yourself with individuals who support your excursion of self-acknowledgment and legitimacy. Establish connections based on mutual respect, trust, and values. Your inner circle ought to be a haven where you can be yourself without worrying about being judged.

Embracing your real self is a ground-breaking excursion—one that starts with grasping your uniqueness, embracing flaws, and developing self-acceptance. You can live authentically and radiate confidence by accepting yourself as you are and loving yourself unconditionally.

In the next chapter, we will delve into the world of fashion and makeup as a means of self-expression. Get ready to show off your style and discover the amazing ways that makeup and fashion can help you feel empowered and uplifted. We'll give you the tools you need to express yourself and tell your story in your own unique way.

Keep in mind, you are an amazing powerhouse. So, with a girl-boss attitude, celebrate your individuality, acknowledge your flaws, and unconditionally accept yourself. You are the first step on the path to authenticity and self-love. You can make your life reflect who you are as an extraordinary person.

Journal Prompts

OMG, girls. Life gets overwhelming sometimes, but we've got this! Consider the following suggestions as starting points for self-reflection and personal development:

- Acquaint yourself with yourself; you can only emphasize the positive aspects!

- What is an apparent shortcoming you accept you have? Make a list of three ways this weakness actually serves as a strength.

- How would it feel to present yourself more thoroughly? What might that resemble?

Don't forget that keeping a journal can provide my precious young girls with a therapeutic outlet where they can authentically express their thoughts, feelings, and experiences. You can deepen your self-reflection and begin a journey of self-discovery by utilizing these prompts.

Putting It All Together

- Take pride in your individuality and the qualities that set you apart.

- Convert comparison into inspiration and allow the accomplishments of others to reignite your own fire.

- Accept flaws as opportunities for self-improvement and growth.

- By acknowledging your worth and accepting all aspects of yourself, you can practice self-acceptance.

- Establish a supportive inner circle, cultivate self-compassion, and shut out your inner critic.

The power of fashion and makeup to express oneself will be discussed in the following chapter, empowering you to embrace your individual style and unleash your creativity.

Key Takeaways

You have taken the first step toward embracing your authentic self, so congrats! In this chapter, we looked at the liberating process of realizing your uniqueness, accepting your flaws, and cultivating self-acceptance. Here is what Sabrina said about embracing her authentic self:

"Prior to getting more ideas of embracing myself, I was continually attempting to squeeze into society's form of what it means to be 'awesome.' I was under the impression that I had to live up to other people's expectations and that my flaws were something to be ashamed of. In any case, subsequent to plunging into the freeing ideas of embracing myself, tolerating my blemishes, and developing self-acknowledgment, I feel like a weight has been taken off my shoulders.

I now know that my superpower is my uniqueness. I never again want to conceal my peculiarities or change myself to satisfy others. Instead, I've begun to accept my flaws as a beautiful part of my identity. It's been an excursion of self-revelation and self-strengthening.

I've gained a new sense of self-esteem and confidence through this process. I now know that mental and emotional health go hand in hand with self-love and acceptance. I presently comprehend that I genuinely deserve love and regard it similarly as I am, with blemishes and all.

I have embarked on a journey of self-discovery and self-acceptance after reading this chapter, which has opened my eyes. I'm thankful for the direction and support to embrace my legitimate self. It's an excursion that I will embrace with fervor and confidence. Much thanks to you for engaging me to venture out and assisting me with the understanding that I genuinely deserve love and acknowledgment, similarly as I am."

Always remember that being genuine is a superpower, and by accepting who you really are, you can open the doors to self-love and personal development.

As we adventure into the following section, prepare to jump into the thrilling universe of fashion and makeup. We will find out how these methods of self-expression can help you become more confident and enable you to share your story. The best is yet to come, my friend. So, get excited!

Chapter 2:

Taking Ownership of Your Actions

Accountability separates the wishers in life from the action-takers that care enough about their future to account for their daily actions. –John Di Lemme

Do you ever feel like you are in the spotlight with all eyes on you? Yeah? That's okay! That's what teenage life is all about. It's the time in your life when every decision you make and every action you take feels magnified. The pressure to fit into societal standards or to please others is sometimes so overwhelming. But you know what? You have the power to take charge and shape your own destiny. Accountability! Yes, that's the secret weapon, my girl. It's time to unleash its magical powers and win the world.

Hey there! Welcome to the next chapter of the self-fulfillment journey that we've started. This chapter is all about owning up to your actions and embracing the power of accountability. I guarantee you that at the end of this chapter, you'll be empowered enough to take responsibility for your actions and choices and cultivate a stronger sense of self-worth and confidence through accountability.

Imagine you're standing on a sparkling stage, bathed in a spotlight that captures your every move. The world is eagerly waiting to witness the unfolding of your unique story. You're the star of your own story, and this role comes with significant power and responsibility. So, are you ready to dive into the exciting world of accountability? Let's discover how accountability can transform your life for the best.

Understanding Accountability

Accountability? What is it? You might think it's a big word, but if you are familiar with the word responsibility, you would surely know what accountability is because both words reside within the realm of synonyms. Here, I'll introduce you to the concept of accountability in detail, and you'll see how this is going to bring a constructive change in your life!

Let's begin with unraveling the basic idea of accountability.

Accountability is accepting responsibility for your choices, decisions, and actions. It is a trait of being responsible and open to making choices and decisions. Accountability isn't just admitting that you're wrong; it's about realizing that you hold power over your own life. When you take charge of your behavior and action, you become an active participant in your journey of self-development.

Accountability means that you acknowledge that what you do impacts yourself and the people around you. When you hold yourself accountable, you're not just being honest with other people, but you're being sincere to your own self.

Let's uncover how you can be accountable toward yourself and those around you.

Being Accountable to Yourself

Self-accountability is something that we all need in our life. It requires self-awareness, self-reflection, and willingness to accept your strengths and weaknesses. Though we all know how important it is, we still make excuses, right? If you want self-accountability in your life, here is what you need to work on.

Being Intentional

Self-accountability isn't something that you develop overnight. It's not a genetic trait that falls magically onto your lap. It requires a lot of effort, which I'm sure you're up to making, right?

To practice accountability, you need to cultivate mindfulness in your life, which means being fully aware of one's thoughts, feelings, and actions. It enables you to pause, reflect and assess the consequences of your choice before action. Other than being mindful, intentionality is also important in practicing self-accountability.

It involves conscious awareness that directs one's actions toward the desired outcomes. You might be wondering how I'm going to practice mindfulness and intentionality. It might seem like something huge, but trust me, all you need is consistency, and you'll ultimately achieve self-accountability.

Self-accountability is a process of constantly keeping yourself updated about your commitments and goals. It's like telling yourself to be responsible even if no one is around.

Let me tell you something to make the concept of self-accountability a little easier for you to understand. During my high school days, I had a big project due in two weeks. It was research work that required a lot of time and effort.

As the days went by, I was distracted by social media, video games, and hanging out with friends. But then, something clicked in my mind, and I realized that only one week was left, no one else was going to meet my deadline, and I would fail the course.

Then, I immediately started working on it. I made a schedule, set the hours for research, and then wrote several paragraphs and reviewed them afterward. I resisted all my temptations to procrastinate. Throughout the week, I remained committed to my project, and finally, when the day arrived, I submitted my project and felt a deep sense of satisfaction and pride.

So, my dear, it's all about the realization that only you are responsible for your future. So, get up and make it bright!

Freeing Yourself from the Blame Game

Have you ever heard of excusitis—the failure disease? It happens when you constantly blame your circumstances, society, and people for your failure. If you find yourself doing this often, you need to work on it. You don't have to get worried; just relax because we all do this at some point in our lives. All you have to do is to realize this weakness. Once you've self-realized, it becomes easy to correct it.

Accountability is all about taking charge of your success as well as failure and letting go of excuses. And let me tell you that 85% of the consequences of your actions depend on you, not on your surroundings. I once read a quote that I would like to share; it went like this:

You can blame people for placing you behind a door, but blame yourself for staying behind the door.

So far, this has helped me in my self-accountability journey, and I really hope it helps you too.

Being Accountable to Others

Being accountable to others refers to being responsible and committed toward the obligations and promises in relationships with another individual. It includes the recognition of the impact of your actions on those around you. When you're accountable to others, you prioritize open communication, trust, and reliability. Also, it requires a sense of integrity and respect.

It Requires a Sense of Openness

A sense of openness comes when you willingly share your goals with someone else, for instance, with your trusted friend or mentor. If you're an introvert or have a reserved nature, it might take a little longer to open up, but that's okay! Everything takes time, right? So, don't worry, you'll eventually come around sooner or later.

Define a Clear Goal

When it comes to being accountable to others, obviously, it involves someone else in your life journey. So, you've to ensure that your goals are clearly defined and specific. No one wants to burden another person with their insecurities, fears, and doubts. So, will you, right?

It's completely okay not to have a certain goal, but you can have a little sense of direction and be aware of where you're now and how far you want to go.

This accountability thing might sound like too much work to do, but my girl, let me tell you one thing: no one is born to be accountable. It's a skill that is only acquired with patience, practice, and consistency. So, hey, you got it!

We're talking so much about accountability, self-accountability, and accountability to each other. But why is it so crucial? Well, it is because of the fundamental element of personal growth. Accountability always has a space for self-improvement, learning from mistakes, and leads you to become a better version of yourself.

Let me tell you a story about my friend, Maya. Maya was a brilliant student who always strove for excellence in her academics. It was our exam week; unfortunately, Maya prepared the biology instead of the chemistry exam. She said I was so sure that it was a biology exam. Her over-surety leads to this!

It was a huge thing for her. She was panicking and crying but somehow managed to take the exam. Even though she secured good marks in the end, she felt so disappointed in herself. She couldn't believe that she had made such a big mistake. But instead of dwelling on her disappointment, she decided to learn from it and will review the exam schedule before preparing rather than relying on her surety.

What Happens When a Teen Dodges Responsibility for Their Action?

If you still aren't motivated enough to make efforts to start practicing accountability, let me tell you some of the consequences that can arise as a result:

- **Relying on Others:** If you do not take responsibility for your actions, you will start relying on other people for your happiness and entertainment, which is definitely not good for my girl's personal growth, right?

- **Strained Relationships:** Avoiding accountability creates a huge gap between relationships with family, friends, and loved ones. It erodes trust and can lead to disappointment.

- **Stunted Emotional Intelligence:** Lack of accountability can hinder the development of emotional intelligence, as it involves understanding one's emotions and their impact on others. Taking responsibility fosters empathy and helps develop interpersonal skills.

- **Missed Growth Opportunities:** By dodging accountability, you'll miss out on the chance to learn from your mistakes, develop resilience and build a stronger sense of self.

- **Limited Problem-Solving Skills:** By not facing the consequences of your action, you might miss the opportunity to learn how to identify and address the challenges life gives you, find solutions for your problems, and make better decisions in the future.

- **Reinforced Negative Pattern:** Constantly avoiding accountability can reinforce negative behavior patterns. As a teen, this isn't good for you at all. It can perpetuate the cycle of irresponsibility and restrain your ability to break free from negative habits.

Nobody wants these inabilities in their life, right? You know what; I've got a story to tell you that will surely help you to start taking accountability for your actions from today.

Back when I was in high school, there was this totally rad student named Liza. She loved acting and always took part in school plays. Liza wanted to direct her own play, but she had trouble staying organized and meeting schedules, which kept her from reaching her full potential. It really hurt her hopes of becoming a director.

But Liza decided one day that enough was enough. She finally decided to show the world and herself what she was capable of doing. She decided it was time to take care of her life and use her creative abilities. Liza knew that she needed a good plan if she wanted to do well.

With her idea in mind, Liza got her friends who were interested in action and made her own cast and crew. She started making a schedule for putting on the play. She carefully planned out the times for rehearsals, the dates for building the set, and the times for costume rehearsals. She ensured everyone was on the same page and knew what their jobs were.

Of course, it wasn't always easy to stay on task. Along the way, Liza had to deal with distractions and sometimes had questions. But she got in touch with her inner director and stuck to her goal. She didn't put off her play or get distracted by other things. Instead, she put it first and made sure everything was on track.

Liza realized that taking responsibility meant reflecting on her actions, accepting feedback, and seeking guidance from those around her. So, she talked to her acting teacher often and asked her fellow students for feedback. She listened to their suggestions, was open to constructive feedback, and made the changes needed to improve the show.

Liza saw her play come to life as the practices went on. The players gave strong performances, the sets were made with care, and the costumes gave the stage a touch of magic. Liza was full of joy and nerves as she stood backstage on the day of the show.

As the curtains went up and the story unfolded in front of the crowd, Liza felt a huge sense of pride and accomplishment. Her play was a hit, and everyone admired her work. But more than just being liked by other people, Liza felt a rush of self-esteem and confidence that lit up the room. She knew in her heart that she had made her dreams come true by taking charge of her life.

Liza's experience taught her how important it is to be responsible for herself and how that can help her reach her goals. She made her idea come true by staying organized, staying on task, and being open to working with others.

Her story turned into an inspiration, which encouraged other students to take responsibility for their own work. Liza had shown them that "accountability" wasn't just a boring buzzword; it was a secret weapon that could help them reach their goals and their full potential.

So, gorgeous, let Liza's story remind you that you can take responsibility for your actions; you become the boss babe of your own life.

Accountability isn't about putting limits or restrictions on yourself. Instead, it's about giving yourself the power to rise above problems and shine like the supernova you are. So go out into the world, find your inner Liza, and make your own masterpieces that will make everyone gasp. You got this, girl!

Building Accountability Skills

Now that we understand how important accountability is, let's explore some of the practical strategies that will help you develop the essential accountability skill which is crucial for your personal growth and development.

Accepting and Acknowledging Others' Accountability

Just like you're responsible for your actions and choices, so are others. You don't have to take responsibility for everyone's actions. Just embrace the idea that people are accountable for what they say and what they do. Appreciate each other's accountability and create a supportive environment that helps you in personal growth and development. It also inspires others to take charge of their actions.

Understand That Everyone Makes Mistakes

Understand that we're not responsible for everything that happens in our lives. Sometimes unfortunate things happen, and there's nothing we can do about it. Mistakes are a natural part of life. They don't define who you are; in fact, they just provide you with the opportunities to grow and learn new experiences in your life.

It's crucial to understand that everyone makes mistakes, but how to deal with them depends on you. So instead of beating yourself up over these mistakes, try to focus on the positive side and extract valuable lessons from them. Keep my words in mind "Each mistake you make is a stepping stone toward personal development."

Own Your Mistakes

Owning your mistakes is nothing but a superpower! It takes a lot of courage to admit and accept that you've made a mistake. And it's okay to make mistakes; no one is perfect. Even the most honest people sometimes make mistakes.

All you have to do is learn from them and own them. It shows maturity, integrity, and genuine commitment to self-improvement (Hattie & Timperley, 2007). So now that my girl-there is no such thing as a mistake, there are only lessons!

Okay, picture this: My friends and I decided to have a little spa day on a sunny Saturday afternoon at my house. We had facial masks and cucumbers for our eyes, and we even took a shot at giving each other a massage. How cool! We thought we were living in a scene from a chick flick because it was all giggles and laughter.

I considered myself a master in nail art, so I confidently proposed to paint everybody's nails. I brought out my assortment of vibrant nail polishes as we all gathered around the coffee table. I began with my dearest companion, Emma. I was determined to make her nails look flawless because she wanted a vibrant pink to match her outfit.

Here's where the unexpected scene occurred: My hand suddenly twitched as I applied the first coat of pink polish, which penetrated far beyond her nail and onto her skin. I let out an awkward laugh as my heart dropped, hoping Emma wouldn't be too upset.

"*Goodness, Emma, Please accept my apologies!*" Trying not to panic, I said. "A*llow me to fix it.*"

Rather than attempting to deny my mistake, I chose to take ownership of it. I admitted, "*Okay, I messed up,*" taking a deep breath in and looking Emma in the eyes. Emma, I'm so sorry.

Emma exclaimed with surprise and laughter, easing the tension in the room. She said, "*No worries, girl,*" wiping away tears of laughter, "*It's just nail polish. We can clean it later. Furthermore, it's an interesting memory we will always remember!*"

Furthermore, very much like that, the "nail art disaster" transformed into a bonding moment between my girls. As soon as we all shared our own epic beauty blunders, my mistake suddenly felt less embarrassing. In fact, it became a treasured friendship memory.

Accepting my faults instructed me that it's okay to screw up at times, and it doesn't make me any less skilled or adorable. I learned that being real and genuine is what truly matters, so I stopped trying to be perfect. It demonstrated to my friends that I was willing to take responsibility for my actions and grow from them.

Don't Blame Others Because You're in Denial

When we don't want to accept responsibility for our actions, we often blame the other person. But listen up,ignoring the truth won't help. You must be careful not to start seeing other people as easy scapegoats for your own mistakes. Placing the blame on another person is the first step in a vicious cycle that will never end well for anyone.

Taking responsibility for your actions and the consequences of those actions is the only way to break this cycle and move on to making better choices in the future. It's time to stop making excuses and start owning up to your mistakes. Accept the unsettling reality and let it push you toward greater maturity.

See the Value in Your Responsibilities

Let me tell you a little secret—responsibilities are not as bad as they seem! In fact, they can be pretty awesome! When we take on responsibilities, we are allowed to grow and learn new things. It may seem difficult at first, but once we take that first step, we realize that we are capable of so much more than we thought. So, don't be afraid of responsibilities.

They give meaning and purpose to your life, shape your personality, and help you to grow. They make life worth living and give a reason to get up in the morning. Without them, life would be dull and meaningless. So, my friend, if you don't want to live a dull life, start seeing value in your responsibilities.

Cultivating Accountability

These strategies helped me to become accountable in my life. By practicing these strategies, you can strengthen your accountability skills as well. Remember that building accountability is a continuous process that requires honesty, self-reflection, and willingness to learn and grow.

Starting today and over time, sooner or later, you will gradually develop a strong sense of personal responsibility and become a more accountable and empowered woman!

Developing a Sense of Responsibility

Here is how I, myself, became a girl who developed a sense of personal responsibility. I arranged a bake sale for charity. I also gathered a group of enthusiastic volunteers to assist me with it. We divided up the tasks, came up with a list of delectable baked goods, and thought of ideas. I was in charge of ensuring that everything ran smoothly and coordinating the logistics. We were determined to cheerfully serve everyone despite the excitement and chaos.

Boom, one of the workers coincidentally thumped over a plate of newly baked treats, sending them crashing onto the floor. I could feel the weight of the situation on my shoulders as the room fell silent briefly. It would have been not difficult to fly off the handle and point fingers; however, all things being equal, I took a full breath and got a move on.

While the rest of us continued to serve customers, I quickly rallied the team and assigned someone to clean up the mess. We didn't allow that incident to dampen our spirits. We knew that errors would occur, but how we handled them was the most important factor.

I learned the value of teamwork and responsibility from that bake sale. It showed me that, as young people, we could have a beneficial outcome on our general surroundings. Each responsibility we accept shapes us into capable and compassionate individuals, whether it's organizing an event, volunteering in our community, or taking on leadership roles.

In this way, my kindred girl, you can change things. With open arms, accept responsibility, and watch as you develop into the amazing person you were meant to be!

The Link Between Accountability and Self-Esteem

When it comes to accountability, the first thing it boosts in you is your self-esteem and confidence. Now why are they related to each other, and how does accountability help nurture self-esteem? Let's explore the powerful connection between them!

When you take charge of your actions, you show a deeper level of self-respect and integrity. By taking responsibility, you build trust in yourself and in other people. Accountability plays a crucial role in boosting our self-esteem as well as our level of confidence.

Accountability makes you the architect of your own destiny. You no longer rely on approval or validation for others to feel good about yourself because you know where you're heading in your life, and your actions are more important than anyone's words.

Accountability sets you free from the shackles of self-doubt and insecurities. You start believing in yourself, making you the star of your own story. It gives you the courage to unapologetically start owning your choices and follow the path toward success (Guindon, 2002).

Why Accountability Matters to Self-Esteem?

The teenage years are when you boost your self-esteem to the next level by embracing accountability. Why? Let's acknowledge the importance of accountability through this testimonial by Elena, who is 15 years old and lives in my neighborhood:

"Being held accountable has fundamentally altered my life. Admitting when I've failed or made a mistake isn't always easy, but accepting responsibility has improved my self-esteem. At the point when I consider myself responsible, I take responsibility for activities and decisions. It shows that I esteem myself and my development. I confront the consequences head-on rather than blaming the other party or making excuses. Not only has this increased my self-esteem and confidence, but it has also earned me respect from others. Realizing that I have the ability to offer to set things straight and improve permits me to explore existence with a feeling of direction and honesty. Accountability is important because it enables us to be our best selves and truly believe in our abilities."

We learn to ride out the storm: We all mess up sometimes, but don't worry! It's just a bump in the road, ya know. We'll get through it and come out even stronger. Sometimes mistakes can be a total bummer when we don't get what we want or have to do stuff we don't feel like doing.

But, mistakes don't define us, and we can totally learn from them to become even better versions of ourselves. We learn to say, "This is the result of what I've done, and I know how to handle it." The more we make mistakes, the more we enhance the ability to get through life.

We learn to accept our process: Do we punish a child who is learning to walk every time they fall? Absolutely not! We know that falling down is part of learning to walk. We don't see it as a failure but as part of the process. It's amazing how we cheer on children as they learn and grow, yet we can be so hard on ourselves when we make mistakes.

Let's remind ourselves of the same kindness and encouragement we give to the children. After all, we're all just works in progress! Isn't it amazing how we continue to learn and grow, even as we get older? Our mistakes may not be as dramatic as they were in our youth, but they still show that we are putting ourselves out there and trying new things.

Keep up the great work! Holding ourselves accountable means that we happily admit our mistakes as a part of the learning process and as a sign of our desire to keep growing, learning, and living.

We learn self-forgiveness: One of my teachers used to tell me that "90% of you is not your 10% best." In simple words, even if you give your best, there's still so much that is imperfect. Hey there! It's totally normal to feel like you're not quite perfect, even when you're giving it your all. But guess what? That's what makes you unique and special!

It's amazing how much easier life becomes when we take responsibility for our actions. We learn to let go of the need to be perfect and instead focus on learning and growing. The lessons and experiences that come from being wrong can be just as valuable, if not more so, than the satisfaction of being right.

We learn to self-advocate: It's not always our fault. Everyone has experienced the anger and frustration that comes from being unfairly blamed; just lately, I had to deal with a manager who blamed a coworker's conduct on me.

Being comfortable with accountability allows us to recognize the situation where we're not responsible, as our "accountability meter" is more precise. We learn to stand our ground and have straight, honest confrontations with people who like to point fingers.

Journal Prompts

Now it's time to do some activity and see how far we have come. So, grab your journal, and let's explore some thought-provoking prompts:

- Write down the goal you want to achieve and the steps that you need to take to ensure you hold yourself accountable throughout the journey. Visualize your success and how good it will make you feel to take responsibility for your action.

- Describe a mistake you made and what you learned from it. How can you use what you've learned to ensure greater accountability in the future? Think about how much you've grown when you admit your mistakes and use them as stepping stones.

- Reflect on any recent situation where you took ownership of your action. How did it make you feel? Embrace the power of owning up to your decisions and how it helps boost your self-esteem.

Putting It All Together

Here's the main crux of the chapter that you can note down in your journal:

- Accountability is taking responsibility for your choices and actions.

- It's the primary element for personal growth and continuous improvement.

- Own your actions with courage and integrity.

- See mistakes as an opportunity for growth and learning

- Don't blame others for your actions

- Embrace others' accountability to build supportive and healthy relationships.

- Accountability boosts your self-esteem and lifts your confidence.

Key Takeaways

Great job, you! Great job on taking a huge step toward personal growth! It's amazing to see you embracing the power of accountability. Just wanted to remind you that every choice you make has the power to shape your future positively. You're setting yourself up for a bright and empowered life by taking ownership of your actions. Keep up the great work!

I'm so excited for the next chapter! We will explore the amazing world of self-expression and how to overcome your fears. It's time to show off your unique style and let your inner beauty shine! Grab your favorite lip gloss and get ready to express yourself like the amazing person you are!

Before we move on, let's take a moment to reflect on the amazing journey you've embarked upon! Reflect on the moments when you've shown courage and accountability by taking responsibility for your actions. You've got this. Just wanted to remind you of the amazing growth and self-assurance that you've achieved. You've come so far and should be proud of yourself. Get ready for the next chapter—it's going to be epic!

Chapter 3:

Exploring Trends and

Igniting Confidence

Happiness and confidence are the prettiest things you can wear.
—Taylor Swift

I couldn't agree more with Taylor! The universe smiles when you smile, and the world laughs when you laugh. Your confidence is what makes you stand out in the crowd, my girl.

Seriously, most of the time, when anybody tries to make you feel bad, in fact, they are the ones who are insecure about themselves. That's them projecting their negative energy onto you, which has nothing to do with you!

On this note, let's begin the third chapter by becoming a confident version of yourself. In this chapter, we'll dive deep into the realm of self-acknowledgment so that you can boost your confidence level and adopt new fashion trends to be the hottest yet coolest lady in the town.

Thus, prepare to plunge into a universe of patterns and recognize your innate powers. We will investigate the most recent fashion styles, overcome the anxiety toward judgment, and accelerate your confidence more than ever in this chapter.

As for now, we will cut to the chase. It's time to show everyone that you have got the Midas touch. Do not feel reluctant to express your true self by exploring trends. Read on.

Challenging the Insecurities of People

Let's spill the tea, girl. At times, you are surrounded by insecure people who always pull you down and make you feel lower about yourself. Listen to me on this. It is unwise to care about such people. Neither are their opinions about you. Even if it's someone from your close friend's list, ignore them.

Guess why? Because they are insecure about their own selves, which is the only reason they try to put negativity in your life. They need to have a life outside of these insecurities. They need to fix themselves, not you!

Get this through your head, and don't you ever forget this: Secure and confident people do not waste time tearing other people apart!

They're too preoccupied with living their lives; however, those who constantly criticize or judge. You see, they're just fighting their internal demons. Let them be!

Dealing With Their Negative Comments

If somebody is trying to make you feel bad by commenting on your makeup, hair, dress, looks, or anything, make sure you don't let their negative comments get to your head. Never allow them to ruin your day.

Their negative comments about you are nothing but them spilling their insecurities. Remember, mere words should not dim your sparkle. For that, you're just too amazing.

Keep in mind that their judgments are not about you at all, so resist the urge to internalize their rude comments. It's their inaccurate approach to addressing their own problems. So, take a chill pill.

I kid you not, gals; I myself have suffered from the negative comments of people in my teenage years.

Envision this situation: I am happy and proud of my new hairstyle as I enter school. I've invested the energy to experiment and express my exceptional hair-style. However, when I enter the passage, I hear murmurs and negative remarks about my hair from a gathering of fellows.

At that time, I felt an ache of self-uncertainty and weakness. I remember stopping for a while and thinking for a minute: *"Their negative remarks are more indicative of them than of me. Their own insecurities and struggles with self-acceptance are the source of those remarks. They are attempting to bring me down to their level by projecting their negativity onto me."*

However, I know that I am far too amazing for their comments to dim my sparkle. I understand that their comments don't characterize my value. Then, I strolled past them, advising myself that their cynicism wasn't my weight to bear.

Keep in mind, young ladies, we are able to pick whose opinion matters. Encircle yourself with positive impacts who inspire and uphold you. Never let anyone's negative remarks ruin your day. Keep shining your light and embracing your uniqueness. Keep your integrity and allow their comments to pass you by like water off a duck's back.

Push Away the Pessimism

Did you know? You have the power to keep your circle positive and full of love. Their negativity should not define your personality or your life in any way. Take a deep breath, shake it off, and continue to kill. You are similar to a sparkling star, and their insignificant feelings can't diminish your light, not even for a second. Ignore the pessimism.

Realize Your Worth, Love!

Focus on the main thing, bae. Encircle yourself with inspirational vibes and individuals who lift you. Create a group of ferocious friends who will celebrate you for the amazing person you are. Because, honey, you deserve the world!

Let Go of Your Frenemies

Are you fed up with stressing over your friends roasting you? Are you high-key hesitant to speak your heart out? Well, girl, don't worry. I've got your back. We will confront those fears head-on, easing your fear of being judged and stepping into your spotlight of self-assurance.

Say No to Toxic Friends!

I've had this companion who appeared to be pleasant on a superficial level, yet I was unable to shake off the uncomfortable inclination whenever I was around her. Something really didn't add up about our dynamic. At some point, I understood that I deserved a better friend. It happened when my teacher gave me full marks on a test, and she got lower marks.

That day, she stayed angry with me, and I started feeling so bad about getting good marks. I mean, what kind of friend does that? No, I deserved friends who truly encouraged and supported me, not those who made me feel inadequate or doubted my worth. It was time to part ways with this unhealthy friendship and make room for new relationships that shared my values.

However, it was difficult. Courage was required to confront my doubts about being judged and step into my own spotlight of self-assurance. In any case, I realized that my prosperity and confidence were in question. In this way, I gathered up the solidarity to have a genuine discussion with her and communicated what her remarks meant to me.

Although the discussion didn't go as flawlessly as I thought, it was a turning moment in my life. I made space for new companionships by letting her go which was based on trust, regard, and certifiable help.

Exploring Your Creative Side

And what's more? Fashion is not our only focus. We'll let your creative side out because we believe that imagination has no limits! Get ready to channel your inner artist and let your true self shine through, whether it's through dancing, writing, painting, or any other creative outlet. You are the trend that people aim to follow, so take pride in you being a starter of trends!

I understand that taking the first step toward exploring new trends comes with some challenges, especially those unpleasant judgments. So, sit tight, as now I will take stock of ways to overcome the fear of judgment!

Overcoming the Fear of Judgment

OMG, yeet! We've all been there: feeling completely judged, insecure, and like everyone is scrutinizing us. Isn't it the absolute worst feeling ever? It surely is.

Regardless, believe me when I say that you are not alone, and together we will overcome and rise above the fear because I'll help you win this fear forever.

As for now, are you holding back from wearing your favorite dress just because people keep throwing shade at you? My girl, do not let the opinion of someone else affect you in any way. Keep in mind that the only opinion that matters is your own.

- Accept your worth.

- Love yourself unconditionally.

- Let those who despise you sit back and watch.

- Own that you're way too preoccupied with being fabulous and living your best life!

So, be who you are, rock your individuality, and don't let anyone undermine your self-confidence. Because no one does it better than you. You just have to keep shining like a superstar.

Here is a glowing testimonial from my own sister Alice.

"When I was a teenager, I was extremely self-conscious and afraid that other people would judge me. I struggled to express my true self and pursue my passions due to my fear of ridicule or criticism. I continually stressed over what others would think about me, whether it was my appearance, my decisions, or my fantasies.

Yet, at some point, I reached my limit. I realized that I was the only one who stood in the way of my own happiness and success. I attempted to break free from the shackles of dread and embrace my uniqueness.

It was difficult initially, not going to lie. Getting out of my comfort zone implied dealing with my most profound weaknesses directly. However, I experienced a new sense of liberation and empowerment with each small step I took. I began expressing my real thoughts, chasing after my inclinations, and defending what I had confidence in.

People still didn't stop, lol. However, I quickly realized that their perspectives did not define me. How I saw myself and how much I valued my own worth were the most important factors.

Eventually, I saw a change inside myself. I built genuine relationships with people who valued me for who I truly was because I let go of my fear of being judged and accepted who I was as I was. I found a group of like-minded people who helped and encouraged me.

As of right now, I continue to carry on with my life proudly, commending my peculiarities, interests, and uniqueness. I no longer allow the fear of being judged to prevent me from living my authentic life and pursuing my dreams."

Therefore, my fellow teenagers, I urge you to let go of the fear of being judged and embrace your individuality. You encapsulate mind-blowing potential, and the world has the right to see the genuine you. Remember that you deserve love, acceptance, and success by following your passions. Try not to allow anybody to diminish your light or keep you down. The world is awaiting your genuine brilliance, and you are capable of greatness."

Do you ever wonder what is the mindset of these judgmental people? It's food for thought, so let's take a look at what causes people to judge others in the first place!

The Psychology Behind the Fear of Judgment

You are not alone if you have ever worried that failing an evaluation will cause a friend or coworker to have a bad opinion of you. These feelings are referred to as a "fear of negative evaluation" by psychologists.

In 2015, Indian psychologists reported that students with high levels of anxiety or fear of a negative evaluation were more likely to perform poorly (Ganesh et al., 2015). My lovelies must be wondering what the psychology behind all this is. Let's dig into this beef:

It Develops in Childhood

Do you know that we have been afraid of being judged ever since we were children? Yes, that is correct! Psychologists say that our self-concept and self-esteem develop early because of constant criticism of other people. Confidence hits differently when your parents instill it in you from early childhood. How dope does that sound!

Impact of Negative Judgment on Us

The fear of judgment is a significant barrier to our self-expression and personal growth. In this section, I will explore the roots of this fear and implore strategies to overcome it.

By understanding that the judgments of others are the reflections of their insecurities, you can liberate yourself from their influence and embrace your true self with confidence. It's time to empower yourself to rise above judgment and step into the spotlight of your authentic self.

You Need to Belong

Consider this: I felt cute and ready to slay the dance floor at this cool rave party. However, as soon as I stepped out onto the dance floor, I began to experience these critical glances, as if everyone was whispering about my moves or my attire. It's similar to a moment of buzzkill, and my confidence experienced a plunge. Not so clutch, right?

As a human being, your need for belonging makes you suffer through this fear of judgment. I get you. Our interactive nature is innate. I bet we all have an idea that people are going to talk smack about us. But hold on, boomer! Your opinion is trash if it's affecting my mental and emotional health.

Lowered Self-Esteem

Here is the gag: Judgment has a significant effect on our self-esteem. Constantly worrying about what other people will think can seriously prevent us from being who we are. We develop a fear of differentiating ourselves, trying new things, or accepting our individuality.

Friends, give it some thought. We put ourselves in a small box out of fear of being judged; instead of showing the world who we are, we conform to what society expects of us. Like birds kept in a cage, we are afraid to fly high. But you know what? It's time to let go of that anxiety and soar like queens!

Tada! Now you understand how judgments initiate and why people judge. If you feel lost at sea about what to do about this, let me help you. I am going to mention different strategies to let go of the fear of judgment so you can be yourself. Remember that you are unstoppable!

Strategies to Overcome the Fear of Judgment

Repeat after me: I'm fierce, amazing, and completely open about who I am! The detractors can go sit in a few places while you dominate the game. With an exhilarating level of self-assurance, you will flaunt your individuality, your style, and your quirks!

I understand that's easier said than done. Yet, here's a little stunt: shift your concentration from what others are thinking to your perceptions of yourself. Try not to allow their viewpoints to characterize your value because you are far beyond their shallow decisions, okay?

Become Your Judge

What if you take over the role of the judge from other peeps? To me, this sounds like a plan! Make these three self-care habits a part of your life if you want to be your judge:

- *Self-love:* Be kind to yourself to get past harsh criticism.

- *Self-reflect:* Think about your life to figure out how well you are doing, what are your risky regions, and how you can deal with them.

- *Self-validate:* Instead of seeking approval from others, look for one's approval.

Cooperate With Your Inner Critic

We frequently allow those stares and whispers of criticism to sway us. The cherry on top is we permit them to set off our self-analyzing framework. And as the same thoughts of being judged keep looping in our heads, our self-criticism keeps veering more and more toward negative emotions.

We should make peace with it instead of allowing our inner critic to hinder our peace of mind. Use it to your advantage, girl!

Be There for Yourself

When I say "be there for yourself," I mean that instead of focusing on what people think of you, you should invest in who you are becoming. I'm going to show you a three-step procedure that should help you out here:

Step 1

Create a list of your advantages and disadvantages. If these judgments are false, this will help you reevaluate your position.

Step 2

Focus on yourself. Think about what you want to work on instead of responding to what others have to say about your life. Work on the things that are most important to you and make it a priority.

Step 3

Take care of yourself, strong lady! Appreciate yourself more and concentrate profoundly on developing your abilities. So, you won't have to spend time processing other people's opinions because of this.

Effective Feedback Can Help You Grow!

Constructive feedback is important, so pay attention to it! You might even write down what they say about you. But as you do so, understand that what people say about you does not define who you are, honey. Naturally, you can take their words as something to think about and work on as you pave your way toward growth!

Write Down Affirmations

According to research, writing affirmations can assist in restoring self-esteem and confidence (Cascio et al., 2015). You might be better able to alleviate anxieties about what other people think of you if you recognize your strengths. What other people think of you is unlikely to matter if you are self-assured about your abilities and performance.

I am sure you will shine even brighter if the fear of negative evaluation from others is gone. So, here are a few truths that also come in handy to progress your way toward overcoming the fear of being judged:

Truths to Help You Overcome Your Fear of Being Judged

To assist you in overcoming your fear of being judged, let me enlighten you. Don't forget that I have your back, and together we will conquer this fear like the self-assured queens that we are!

- You are sufficient, similarly, as you are! Repeat after me: "No one's opinion can shake my confidence. I am amazing!"

- I mean, seriously, peeps' perspectives are so meaningless! Why should you care about what other people think? They are unaware of the amazing person you truly are.

- Oh, and the judgments from new acquaintances? Honey, they are brief. Like a late spring fling, they'll suddenly be gone. Individuals' perspectives can change like a breeze, so don't allow them to cut you down.

- A shocking truth awaits you. Positive judgments are possible! Yes, you listened to me, right? You can be lifted, inspired, and made even more fabulous by certain judgments. Embrace those upbeat vibes and let them boost your confidence.

- And what's more? Most people are too preoccupied with their battles to be interested in what you're doing. So, don't worry about other people's thoughts; just rock your style, pursue your interests, and live your best life.

- Buckle up for another shocking truth. A person's judgment is not a measure of their worth; rather, it reflects their insecurities.

- Now, let me tell you a secret. You won't be afraid of being judged if you can stop judging other people. At the point when you embrace a mentality of acknowledgment and understanding, you make a positive judgment space around you.

- Girl, you won't have to worry about being judged at all if you can stop judging yourself. Be delicate with yourself, angel. Appreciate your assets, embrace your peculiarities, and let go of self-judgment.

It's time we unravel the significance of self-expression to recognize how wonderfully it helps enhance confidence in you!

Building Confidence Through Self-Expression

Self-expression is a powerful tool for building confidence and celebrating our individuality. In this section, we will explore various forms of self-expression, such as fashion, art, writing, or any avenue that resonates with your unique personality. By fearlessly expressing ourselves, we unlock a sense of liberation and tap into our inner strengths.

Let me give you a brief overview of what self-expression is to spice things up for you - my confident reader!

Definition of Self-Expression

Self-expression is termed as expressing one's thoughts and feelings, which can be accomplished through words, choices, or actions (Kim & Ko, 2007).

Hello! Prepare to let your creative vibes flow and show the world how ahead of the curve you are. This section is all about expressing oneself and gaining confidence, and believe me, it will be epic!

Types of Self-Expression

Okay homie, you must have an idea of what self-expression is by now. I will illuminate you with the types of self-expression right away!

Expressive Self-Expression

Expressive self-expression means we convey our thoughts, sentiments, and feelings in a solid way that permits us to connect with our peers. This sort of expression can be utilized to create areas of strength for shape with others and is considered positive.

Defensive Self-Expression

In this type of self-expression, we impart our thoughts in a manner that doesn't consider healthy communication or comprehension of ourselves or one another. This sort of demeanor can prompt detachment from the other person because of inaccessible non-verbal communication (like crossed arms) or negative looks. It can likewise prompt more stress and nervousness in our lives.

Self-Expression vs. Free Speech

The right to express one's thoughts and opinions without fear of persecution by government officials for disagreeing with them is known as free speech. How dope!

Self-expression is a form of free speech because it enables us to communicate our thoughts and feelings without fear of persecution from others.

Let's Differentiate Between Free Speech and Self-Expression

When it comes to the difference between free speech and self-expression, self-expression goes beyond words, whereas free speech focuses on expressing ideas, beliefs, and opinions.

It includes a wider variety of creative means of expressing your personality, feelings, and identity. Therefore, self-expression enables you to express who you are as a whole, whereas free speech safeguards your right to express your thoughts.

Have you ever noticed that when we express ourselves authentically, our self-esteem also boosts? It surely does! Do you notice that adrenaline rush in you? If you want to know how, continue reading as we will explore the connection between self-expression and self-esteem.

The Connection Between Self-Expression and Self-Esteem

Your self-esteem will greatly improve if you allow yourself to express yourself. You know what? When you articulate your thoughts, you send a strong message acknowledging and praising your unique character.

This authenticity comes from the inside out and positively affects how you see yourself. It empowers you to navigate life with a fierce sense of self and boosts your confidence like a goddess.

Let's get the ball rolling and explore different styles and trends to show your authenticity!

Exploring New Trends and Styles

Consider this: You are standing in front of your oh-so-stylish closet, which is stocked with both trendy finds and classic pieces. It's like a fashion lover's dream come true, and all you have to do is dive in and make your magic! We will talk about how self-expression and confidence go hand in hand because, girl, when you let your true colors shine, you become an unstoppable force!

Be a Starter in the Fashion Race

Let's discuss being a starter now. It's all about developing the self-assurance to be different and to wear styles that set you apart from the crowd. Embrace the force of taking a stab at a new thing, whether it's pairing two different styles of socks (since who needs matchy?), wearing a boy's jacket like a total style rebel, or going makeup-free to show off your natural beauty. You'll be the talk of the town; people's jaws will drop, and who knows, you might even start a trend that everyone wants to follow!

Fashion Breeds Confidence

But hold on; there's more! It's not just about the clothes, when you use fashion to show who you are. It's about showcasing your unique personality, interests, and passions. It's similar to wearing your heart on your sleeve but with many styles!

So, don't be afraid to rock your favorite rock star's band tee, wear bold prints that exude self-assurance, and accessorize like there's no tomorrow. Let your inner diva shine because your fashion choices reflect who you are.

Self-Expression of a Fashionista

Also, a little secret: Even though looking fabulous is a bonus, fashion is a way to express yourself. It's tied in with taking advantage of your internal power and embracing the certainty that accompanies being consistent with yourself. At the point when you step out in a stellar outfit that mirrors your exceptional style, you emanate confidence and let the world know that you are one wild fashionista!

Fashion That Endures!

Fashion is more than just clothes; it's a great way to show who you are. It's about creating a look that makes you feel like a queen and reflects your personality as well as your uniqueness. So, let's get started and learn how adopting new fashions and trends can boost your self-esteem and confidence.

Moreover, in the next section, we will step into a universe in which we will look into different styles. You can also identify your personal style through this guide, so let's get going!

Exploring Different Styles

Stylist girl, fashion is like a playground full of endless opportunities. It's about keeping an open mind, keeping up with the latest fashions, and daring to try new things with your twist. There is a whole world of fashion for you to explore out there, from the most recent looks from the runway to street style inspiration. Therefore, never be afraid to take risks and be daring and bold. Fashion is all about having fun and being confident in who you are.

I will show you how to find your style as a teenager so that you can be beautiful!

Street Style

Imagine this: You are gliding down the street in a stunning outfit that is drawing attention to itself. Oh no, you aren't just blindly following trends!

You're putting your spin on them and giving them that extra spark that makes people say, "I'm fabulous!" We'll show you how to navigate the world of street style, where individuality takes center stage and fashion becomes an art form.

Traditional Style

The traditional woman is elegant, classy, and refined. She follows a timely and clean style of dressing, enjoys matching outfits, and this is a style that started with men's clothing being simplified and is now widely accepted as the dress code for businesses. Classic people don't care about what's trending right now; they just want to spend money on good and current clothes.

Elegant Style

Derived from the classic design but was more contemporary and casual than the classic design. Fashionable, exclusive clothing in lighter or darker hues. There are no items printed. It should be discrete once if you want to add some prints.

Creative Style

Creative women are always happy, and they like to show it by wearing clothes with ethnic and colorful prints, details, textures, and colors. They are free to create a look reflecting their creativity and individuality because this style makes combining various designs and elements simple.

Your Style is Unmatched

Let's keep in mind something incredible! Your style is timeless, despite the passing of fashion trends. Do not feel compelled to follow every trend simply because it is popular. This is all about cultivating one's sense of self through one's aesthetic.

Trust Your Gut

Accept the fashions that truly move you and make you feel like the fierce queen that you are. Let your instincts guide you and write your fashion manifesto because fashion is all about expressing your taste!

Express Your Personality

So, bae, get ready to rock those outfits and let your fashion choices show how vibrant your personality is. You'll boost your confidence, rekindle your creative side, and demonstrate to the world that you are unapologetically fabulous when you embrace self-expression through fashion!

How about getting some tips on how you can define your style? I am sure it will help you gain a better understanding of your own style.

Tips for Defining Your Style

Do you know that finding your distinctive style is an exciting journey of self-discovery? It's about making a fashion statement that is only yours and confidently expressing who you are. Here are some engaging tips to assist you:

- **Learn about your body:** Girl, make an effort to learn about your body type and the styles that look best on you. Accept your shape and wear clothes that show off your best features, whether you're petite, athletic, or curvy. Keep in mind that confidence is essential for wearing any outfit!

- **Choose the shades that bring you joy:** Colors can elicit feelings and reflect who you are. Pay attention to the colors that resonate most with you as you explore various color palettes. Do vivid colors make you feel alive, or do pastels appeal to you more? Include the colors in your wardrobe that make you feel the most alive.

- **Follow the Fashions That Motivate You:** Begin gathering pictures of styles that get your attention, girl. It could be a retro queen, a minimalist chic goddess, or a bohemian goddess. Mix and match different styles to create a one-of-a-kind combination that reflects your personality. Keep in mind style is about self-articulation!

- **Make a mood board for fashion:** By creating a fashion mood board, you can take your fashion inspiration to the next level. Take some magazines, scissors, glue, and a bulletin board. Arrange on the board the images, patterns, and accessories that speak to you by cutting them out. When it comes to putting together your outfits, you can use this visual representation of your style aspirations as a source of inspiration and assist you in defining your fashion direction.

- **Be sincere and believe in your ideas:** Clouts on social media are a scam. The most valid design proclamations come from deep inside you! Trends that don't match your style or values shouldn't influence you. Be who you are, and let your authentic aesthetic choices shine through.

Fashion Mood Board

It's time to carry out an exciting activity!

- I encourage you to make your own fashion mood board to help you in defining your style. This interactive activity will help you come up with new ideas and organize a set of images and ideas that reflect your fashion sense.

- Take a look at the recent fashion trends. Do they spark interest in you? Let your imagination run wild and seek your style that represents your matchless personality. Rock the world, beautiful, with your extraordinary style and fashion!

Putting It All Together

Yay, look how far we have come! Before we wrap up this part, the following are five major points to direct you toward embracing fashion and lighting confidence:

- Embrace your valid self and let go of the feeling of fear toward judgment.

- Self-expression is an integral asset for building certainty and confidence.

- Fashion is a type of self-expression that permits you to grandstand your independence.

- Stay curious and open-minded, hun! They are critical to investigating recent trends.

- Characterize your own style by knowing your body, picking vibrant tones, and making a mood board of your favorite styles.

Key Takeaways

Kudos for stepping toward achieving your ultimate goal! You now know how to overcome your fear of being judged, grow in confidence by expressing yourself, and try out new fashions and trends.

We will now analyze how our inner circle can significantly affect us! Prepare yourself to embark on a life-changing journey that will enable you to realize your full potential. Keep an open mind and keep an eye on the situation!

Keep in mind that happiness and self-assurance are the most beautiful things one can wear as we move forward on this journey. Therefore, let's take pride in our individuality and work together to navigate the exciting world of self-discovery successfully.

Chapter 4:

Choosing Your Circle of

Influence

Surround yourself only with those who will lift you higher.—Oprah Winfrey

Do you have a squad that's as fabulous as a double rainbow on a sunny day? No? If you're still struggling to make a group of friends who can make your life super amazing, then, this chapter will help you. So, are you excited? We are about to land in the world of choosing your circle of influence.

Here you'll get to know the transformative power of positive influence and empowered friendship can change your life. So, grab your friendship net and get ready to catch some positive vibes out there.

But wait before we start, let me drop a pick-up line that'll make you smile: "Hey, Is your name Google? Because you've everything I've been searching for in a friend." Okay, okay, I know pick-up lines can be cheesy, but sometimes, we need to add a little fun to start the conversation and build new connections.

So, are you ready to curate a squad that has your back and brings the best out of you? You'll see how your choice of friends can shape your future and ignite a journey of personal growth. Let's do this!

Know Who You Want to Be

Knowing who you are and who you want to be is extremely important when making friends. If you want to be a strong, confident, and kind person, hang out with strong, confident, and kind people. I once heard this amazing quote that I would like to share with you:

Show me your friends and I'll tell you your future.

Now imagine you have a friend who restrains your energy. They don't let you reach your goals and always distract you with things that drain your energy and ultimately keep you away from your aims. And now imagine that you have a friend who always encourages you to work on your dreams and tells you to stay focused without being a dictator. So, in this way, you can see what kind of impact you will have on your future!

Surrounding yourself with people with the qualities that you admire can be so uplifting. You'll find that their positive energy rubs off on you, and you'll start to embody those same traits. If you're looking to boost your confidence, hanging out with friends who exude confidence can be really inspiring and uplifting!

Pick Your Friends Wisely

Being picky when it comes to friends is essential. Sometimes, we may think we want to be friends with someone, only to discover that their values and opinions aren't the same as ours.

For instance, you meet someone new and feel that instant connection. But eventually, when you get to know them better, you might find out that they have different values and engage in behaviors that don't align with your own.

But don't worry; it's all a part of the journey of getting to know someone better! It's always good to take a step back and consider whether this person is the kind of friend you want in your life.

Choose friends who share your values, as it leads to a healthier and more uplifting relationship. It's important to surround yourself with people who share your beliefs and inspire you to grow. Choosing your friends wisely can help you build a supportive community that encourages growth and success.

Compliment Others, Build Confidence

Complimenting other people is a kind gesture and a way to build their confidence and self-esteem. When you take the time to truly appreciate those around you, you help to cultivate a positive environment that brings joy to all. It's great to give compliments because they have a boomerang effect. The positivity you put out into the world surely comes back to you (Chubb, 2017).

There is this really close friend of mine named Emily who is incredibly talented at playing the guitar. She has always been passionate about music and spends hours practicing it.

A few months back, Emily invited me to a small gathering where she performed a few songs on her guitar. I was genuinely blown away by her talent and couldn't stop myself from expressing my admiration.

I shared with Emily how amazed I was by her musical abilities, especially her precise finger-picking technique. I could clearly see her face lighten up with joy and pride as I showered her with compliments.

From that moment on, our friendship took on a new level of support and appreciation. Emily felt confident and valued, knowing that someone close to her recognized and admired her talent. She started a page on Instagram as she became more confident in sharing her music with others.

Our friendship thrived because we always gave each other genuine compliments and support.

We developed a strong bond of trust and admiration, which made us feel confident to chase our dreams and cheer each other on for our accomplishments.

I love how our friendship is built on compliments. It's so great to have someone who always brings positive energy and boosts our confidence in all areas of life. So, my girl, never hesitate to compliment your friends. Praise them every day!

Surround Yourself With Positive Role Models

In a world where people often fixate on celebrities and influencers as role models, it's easy to forget that our closest friends can be equally influential in shaping our lives.

As we grow and evolve, our perspective on fictional characters and famous personalities can improve for the better!

I used to have the biggest crush on Edward Elric from Fullmetal Alchemist! I absolutely loved following his journey of self-discovery!

From breaking the rules of alchemy to sacrificing everything for his brother's life, it was truly captivating.

I loved how resilient and determined he was! It's truly inspiring! As I entered a different stage of life, my role models shifted.

Now, I consider my friends as my role models. I'm so lucky to have such amazing friends who inspire me every day! Why? Because they are the ones that genuinely understand and support me.

It's amazing how much our friends can positively impact our lives, even if we don't always realize it. They might not be popular or rich, but just by being themselves, they can inspire us every day.

Think about the times when you admired your friend's sense of fashion or style and bought similar clothes or shoes. Or maybe you repeated something they said to impress your friend when you didn't even know what it meant.

And let's not forget the time you bought something based on your friend's recommendation—guilty as charged! If you can relate to these scenarios, then trust me, your friends are indeed your role models too.

Why Are Friends Incredible Role Models?

Let's have a look at the reasons that make our friend an incredible role model:

We Can Relate to Our Friends

Unlike celebrities, whose lives may be extremely different from ours, our friends typically experience similar challenges and struggles we face. Seeing how they deal with their passions, goals, and everyday problems gives us ideas and motivation to do better in our own lives.

For example, if you've ever watched Naruto, you'll know how much Naruto and Sasuke care about each other and how much they've grown. Their friendship and rivalry were built upon shared life experiences, making their journey more relatable and inspiring.

Our Friends Are Unique

Having a diverse group of friends is quite fortunate, and I'm very lucky in that some of my friends pursued their careers in engineering; some of them decided to go into finance sectors, while others chose doctorate professions.

No matter what your friends are, they can be artists, entrepreneurs, or programmers; they all deserve recognition. Having friends who walk different paths in life is a great opportunity to learn new things, gain new perspectives, and broaden our horizons.

Our friends' achievements and aspirations inspire us to aim higher and reach for the stars as we constantly learn and grow.

Our Friends Are Always There to Help and Give Advice

Our friends are amazing! They not only inspire us, but they also offer valuable advice. It's great to celebrate successes, and it's just as important to seek guidance from those who have achieved their goals when we need help making tough decisions or reaching our own aspirations.

It's amazing how our friends can truly empower us, and their advice is always so valuable. It's always great to seek advice from multiple sources.

I remember when I had my first breakup, my friends were there for me. They helped me cope through the worst phase of my life by sharing their experiences. They didn't just offer advice; they checked up on me regularly and helped me get out of that phase.

Just as our friends are role models for us, so are we for other people. Someone out there admires us for just being who we are, whether we know it or not. As we grow up, it's important to consider how we affect the people around us. What do we want other people to think of us?

Do we want to be seen as unreliable and naive, or as someone who can be counted on and trusted during times of uncertainty?

It's up to you! But just to be clear, I'm not suggesting you should change who you are or act like someone else just to make other people happy. It's all about authenticity.

What I am emphasizing is that our choices and actions have ripple effects, and their effect influences those around us. Understanding this is important for our personal growth and development.

Mindset Determines Role Model Choices

Hey you, I want you to sit for a moment and reflect on your current role model and the aspects of your life that you admire. All done? Now, let me tell you about a recent discovery by our researchers.

They discover that some teens are drawn to positive role models while some are drawn toward negative ones. But why so? The answer, lies in the mindsets that they adopt toward achieving goals.

For example, teenagers who are more likely to be inspired by positive role models usually have a growth mindset. This means they see themselves as active learners and achievers who can accomplish their goals through hard work and perseverance.

With such a mindset, teens strive to achieve their best selves. It's great to see that young people are motivated to be their best selves with this type of mindset! And they look up to us older folk to show them the way.

- Young people with a ***growth mindset*** tend to choose role models who can provide valuable strategies that support their way of thinking.

- When people have a ***prevention mindset***, they tend to choose role models who provide them with prevention strategies.

Here's how positive and negative role models impact your life:

Positive Role Models

Positive role models help young people like you boost their motivation by guiding them to success. They show youth how to achieve their goal and also provide them with a sense of self-worth. Youth with a growth attitude are likely to look up to these kinds of positive role models.

Negative Role Models

Negative role models aren't something bad! They also boost the motivation of young people but in a different way than positive ones. You must be thinking, how? They do so by providing the youth with strategies that help to avoid failure.

They often have personal fears of failure, and it's common for people to fear failure. Negative role models developed ways to overcome it and avoid negative outcomes by using various coping mechanisms and strategies. Young people with a prevention mindset share similar fears, so they look up to them.

Qualities to Look For in a Good Role Model

When looking for a good role model, you can consider several good qualities. It's essential to remain open and receptive to diverse role models you may encounter in your life. Here are some important qualities you can look for in a good role model.

- *Honesty*: Honesty is one of the most important qualities of being a good role model because it forms the foundations of trust and integrity. An honest role model speaks the truth and acts genuinely and transparently.

- *Confidence*: Confidence is contagious. Seeing a confident role model can make you feel more confident in yourself and your skills. People who are confident often have a good outlook and are strong when they face problems. They show that setbacks and failures are brief and can be conquered, encouraging you to think the same way.

- *Responsibility*: Responsibility means taking responsibility for your acts and knowing how they affect you and those around you. A good role model takes their promises seriously and does what they say they will do. Their consistent honesty and righteous behavior make them an inspiration to everyone around them.

- **_Respectful_**: Respect is one of the most essential components of any relationship. A respectful role model treats everyone with respect, no matter how different they are. They value diversity and are open to hearing other points of view. By being kind and empathetic, they create a welcoming and peaceful environment that encourages people to respect each other.

- **_Courage_**: Courage is the ability to face challenges, confront fears and take risks. When a role model shows guts, it encourages others to leave their comfort zones and go after their goals. Their bravery in facing challenges and standing up for what they believe can inspire you to be strong in your own life (Spearman & Harrison, 2010).

Remember, my friend, that this list isn't all-inclusive, and different role models may have other unique characteristics that you can relate to. Look for people who make you want to be the best version of yourself and push you to do so. Ultimately, a good role model should have values and act in ways that are compatible with your own growth and goals.

Nurturing Strong and Empowering Friendships

Friendship during your teenage years can be pretty amazing, but hey there, my girl, I know they can also be challenging sometimes. It is very important to understand the dynamics of these friendships and work to build meaningful connections that empower and support you no matter what. These friendships provide a safe space for sharing, learning, and growing together.

As a teenager, you're in a state of self-discovery, figuring out who you are and where you fit in the world. During this time, friendships or peer relations become extremely important because they provide you with companionship, understanding, support, and a sense of belonging. But here's a thing- friendships, however, aren't always simple; there may be highs and lows and even some drama.

I remember my high school drama, ugh! It was so messed up, honestly. I had this so-called toxic best friend. She was so jealous of my other friends. She always complains about me sharing her secrets with them. Like, can you imagine? Why would I share her secrets with my other friends? But she never believed me.

I created this whole drama involving teachers and our school counselor as well! They believed her because, apparently, she seemed kind and nice but actually was manipulative. When things got out of hand, I decided to end the friendship with her on good terms.

Friendships are often based on similar interests, shared activities, or even appearance. It's natural to be drawn toward people who seem similar to you in any way. But as you grow and learn more about yourself, you'll want to connect with people more deeply. You'll want friends who really know and accept you for who you are and who share your values and goals. Meaningful and real friendships are based on respect, empathy, and without any fear of judgment.

Truths About Friendships

Let's be honest. Friendships can also go through hard times. Conflicts and misunderstandings are normal in any relationship. The key is to communicate with each other openly and honestly. Talk about how you feel and what bothers you while also being a good listener.

Try to see things from your friend's point of view by putting yourself in their shoes. Empathy is the secret to resolving disagreements and strengthening your bond. Understanding certain truths about friendship can help you deal with the problems that come with these relationships:

- ***Perfect friendships are a myth:*** There is no such thing as a perfect friend. Every friendship has flaws; accepting them and working through problems together is important.

- *Friendships take work:* Like any other relationship, friendships need work, communication, and understanding to grow.

- *You have a choice about friendship:* You can choose your friends. You can choose who you hang out with, so make sure you choose people who make you feel good and support you.

- *Friendships are about respecting each other:* Healthy bonds are built on respect for each other. Be nice to your friends and try to understand them.

- *Friendships change and sometimes end:* As people grow and change, so do their friendships. It's normal for some ties to end and new ones to take their place. If any of your friendships ended, it's okay to be sad but don't just stop there.

Ways to Nurture Friendship

Here are some of the practices that you can consider when nurturing and maintaining strong and meaningful friendships:

- *Don't call your friends only when you need them:* You have to reach out to your friend proactively. Check up on them and stay connected.

- **Don't take friendships for granted:** Be thankful and appreciative of the people who help you and lift you up.

- **Help your friends when they're in trouble:** Be there to listen, help, and give them emotional support.

- **Encourage their dreams:** Help your friends pursue their goals and follow their dreams by cheering for them every step of the way.

- **Limit expectations:** Don't forget that everyone has their own lives and responsibilities, so don't put too much pressure on your friends, and always respect their space.

Being a Positive Influence and Uplifting Others

Have you heard about the ripple effect of positive vibes? It's about spreading positive energy and inspiration that seriously make a difference in your life and the lives of people around you!

So, here's the deal, my friend: when you choose to be positive and kind in your relationships, it's like throwing a stone into a calm lake. It makes these amazing ripples that keep going and going. And guess what? These waves not only affect you but also the people around you. What a huge win-win situation!

When you smile at someone or say something nice about them, right away, their day gets better. The best part is that they also reciprocate it, and before you know it, your good energy will make the rest of your day.

By being a positive influence, you not only make yourself feel better, but you also help society to make the world a better place (Teodoro, 2017). Girl, know that you have the power to change your relationships and inspire the people around you.

How Can You Be a Positive Influence?

So, if you decide to be a positive influence in the lives of those around you, I have some juicy tips to share. Here they are:

- **Be Authentic:** First thing first, your amazing authentic self! Never try to be like someone you're not just to please them. Embrace your uniqueness and let your true self shine. Authenticity attracts positivity and genuine connection. Just trust me, it's way cooler to be real than be a copycat.

- **Respond, Don't React:** Here's the secret to remaining chill and calm—respond, don't react. Reacting in the heat of the moment can lead to drama and negativity, but responding deliberately and quietly will bring a wave of understanding and harmony. When something happens or someone says something that ruffles your feathers, take a deep breath and then respond.

- **Don't Judge:** Be welcoming and open-minded to others rather than judgmental. Everyone here is on their own path, right? Accept and embrace the perspective of different viewpoints. Don't forget that you don't have to agree with everyone, but you can choose to learn about them and show them some love regardless of whether or not you agree with them.

- **Never Lie:** The foundation of any trusting relationship is honesty. Being truthful is more appropriate, even if it isn't always easy. People appreciate honesty as it shows them that they can rely on you. So, keep it real and be the honest queen that you are!

- **Be Kind Rather Than Be Right:** Let's prioritize kindness over being right! It's natural to want to express our opinions and have healthy debates, but let's remember to stay positive and open-minded. Trust me, girls, it's always better to be kind than to be right.

- **Actively Listen to What People Are Saying:** Pay attention while someone is talking to you. Always make sure to listen to what the person is saying and show them that you genuinely care. Let them feel that you're curious to hear more about their thoughts and feelings. It feels like sending a warm virtual hug and providing a comfortable environment for them to share their thoughts (Carnegie & Hadi, 2013).

By manifesting these qualities and taking these steps, you can surely influence the lives of those around you. Remember, these small things can make a big difference, so go out there, because it's your time to spread positivity like confetti!

Spreading Positivity Through Compliments

Compliments have an amazing ability to make people feel better and change their lives. When you sincerely appreciate and acknowledge others, boost their confidence and create a ripple effect of positivity. Imagine a world where people actively encouraged and celebrated each other by giving sincere compliments. It would be a place full of self-assurance, kindness, and deep connections (Smith, 2013).

Think about what I told you about my friend Emily's story. By sincerely complimenting her musical ability, I lit a spark in her. People's passions are fueled by compliments, encouraging them to keep going and giving them the confidence to step out of their comfort zones. Not only do they boost confidence, but they also strengthen bonds and make people feel like they belong. When we consistently praise and encourage each other, we create a supportive environment where everyone feels valued and honored.

So, don't be shy about giving compliments. Spread them around like confetti and watch them do their thing. Tell your family, friends, coworkers, and even strangers how great they are. Your words can make someone's day better, give them more confidence, and make them want to reach for the stars. Remember that sincere praises come back to you. The good things you do for others will always return to you. You boost your own confidence and self-esteem by making other people feel good. Let's make it our goal to spread happiness by giving sincere praise. Be a ray of sunshine in someone's life and watch as they light up the world with their happiness.

How to Give Compliments

Here are some of the practical tips for giving sincere compliments and nurturing a culture of positivity.

- **Be sincere when giving a compliment:** First, always aim to provide genuine compliments. If you want your words to have an actual impact, you must be honest.

- **Smile when you give someone a compliment:** Be cheerful when you pay a compliment. Your cheerful expression adds credibility to what you say.

- **Compliment someone on what they are proud of:** Acknowledge their accomplishments or outstanding qualities that they value in themselves.

- **Give specific compliments:** Instead of generic praise, mention specific actions, traits, or efforts that impressed you.

- **Offer compliments without an agenda:** Give compliments without expecting anything in return.

- **Don't make compliments about you:** Focus on the honoree and their accomplishments rather than trying to steal the show.

- **Follow up and expand on your compliments:** Talk about what you liked about it to learn more about it.

- **Don't delay your compliments:** Positive things should be acknowledged and shared promptly for maximum effect (Schroth, 2022). I remember when I was in high school, randomly sitting in the cafeteria. My best friend was absent that day. I was reading a novel, and a girl from my chemistry class came up to me and said, "Hey, I just wanted to tell you that I love your style. Your outfit always looks put together and unique. It's inspiring." Her words made my day, and that day I realized that I should maybe do this too because it just sparkles the other person's day!

Role Model Spotlight

Now, it's time to take out your journal, sit and think about a positive role model that you admire and write about them in your journal. This is a great opportunity to focus on the positive impact that this person has had on your life.

Think about all the amazing qualities, accomplishments, and ways in which they motivate and inspire you. This exercise is a great opportunity to recognize the positive influence that role models can have on your personal development.

Putting It All Together

- Surround yourself with people who inspire you.

- Choose friends who share your values and help you in personal growth.

- Give others sincere compliments to lift up their confidence and foster meaningful connections.

- Look up to positive role models to build relationships with people who embody good qualities.

- Empowering friendship requires respect, effort, and mutual support.

- Be proud of your ability to make a positive change in your relationships and lift others.

- Spread positivity by giving sincere compliments and making kindness a way of life.

Key Takeaways

So far, we've explored the amazing benefits of surrounding yourself with positive and supportive people, cultivating strong and uplifting friendships, and making a difference in the lives of those around you.

When you surround yourself with positive people and believe in your ability to make a difference, you can improve your life and help create a more inspiring world.

Exciting news! The next chapter will explore avoiding peer pressure and setting healthy boundaries. So, get ready for an exciting journey.

Chapter 5:

Resisting Negative Peer

Pressure

To be yourself in a world that is constantly trying to make you something else is the greatest accomplishment. –Ralph Waldo Emerson

Ladies, peer pressure is a topic that is so hyped but oh-so-real. Similar to the overrated film that everyone is raving about, but with real consequences. But don't worry about it because you can say "no" when peer pressure goes against your values. It's time to show off your individuality as the queen that you are!

As you navigate the ups and downs of peer pressure, consider your own rules. What is important to you? What are your beliefs, goals, and dreams?

It becomes much simpler to recognize when peer pressure is not in line with who you are when you have a clear understanding of who you are and what you stand for.

Steer Your Own Boat!

Keep in mind that you have the right to be who you are. Therefore, show the world that you won't be distracted by anything that doesn't align with your fabulous self by embracing your uniqueness and rocking your values. It's time to say goodbye Felicia, to unhelpful peer pressure, and hello to a life that is purely yours.

Pull up a chair while reading it because now we will explore the kinds of peer pressure. The one that puts you in hot water and the other that helps you grow!

Recognizing Positive and Negative Peer Pressure

So, it's time to put on your detective hat and start spotting the signs of negative peer pressure. It could be the persistent urge to try something you dislike or to conform to fit in. You can safeguard your health and make decisions that truly reflect who you are by being aware of these warning signs.

Let me break it down for you, starting with the actual meaning of peer pressure. It's similar to this mysterious force that tries to influence your choices and actions based on what your friends or peers are doing.

Meaning of Peer Pressure

Any positive or negative influence from a peer group is considered peer pressure. This group of friends may be of the same age, like kids in the same classroom. Still, they may also share other characteristics, like being mothers, having professional associations, or living in the same neighborhood.

Peer Pressure in Teens

Do you have any idea how teens are the most affected population due to peer pressure? If not, let's look into some statistics.

Young adults and teens both experience peer pressure, but how these pressures are internalized and expressed can be influenced by gender.

For instance, girls were more likely than boys to report feeling a lot of pressure to look among the 29% of teens who responded that they experienced peer pressure to look "good" (Pugle, 2022).

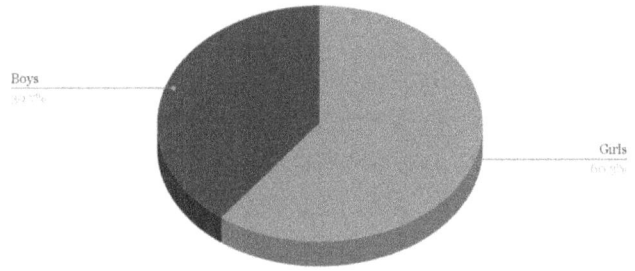

Positive Peer Pressure

Did you know that peer pressure can sometimes lead to amazing experiences and positive transformations? Positive peer pressure is what we mean when your friends push you to be your best self.

It's like your team pushing you to achieve your goals. Most people overlook positive instances of peer pressure, such as situations in which friends encourage teens to grow positively.

One of the most effective ways for a teen to behave well and make wise decisions is through peer pressure.

Consider, for instance, a teen who is surrounded by peers that are members of an academic club, a group that participates in class and strives for good grades.

Can you imagine positive peer pressure can do wonders and nourishes your personality in so many ways? Trust me, it does. When I think back about my high school time, I see how positive peer pressure helped me so much both academically and personally. Observe on your own in the given example of my school study group:

I was a member of a study group in high school, where we supported and encouraged one another to succeed academically. We accepted constructive and positive peer pressure as we prepared for a hard math test. We participated in friendly rivalry, shared different methods to solve a math problem, and praised each other's accomplishments. I learned from this experience how important it is to surround oneself with inspiring peers who encourage us to do better. Positive peer pressure can drive us to accomplish more, get out of our comfort zones, and tap into our maximum capacity. Search out companions who elevate and consider you responsible, making a circle of impact that impels everybody toward progress and self-awareness.

Negative Peer Pressure

However, let's not overlook the other side of the coin. Peer pressure that is bad for you is like that annoying little devil on your shoulder that makes you want to do things that you know aren't right for you. It could be doing something risky like using drugs or not going to school.

When you're under pressure from your peers, it's important to remember your values and learn to say "no." Trust me when I say standing up for yourself is the greatest achievement. It's not always easy.

Consider, for instance, I had a sophomore transfer student, Mike, in my class who faced trouble making friends in class, except for this cool guy who welcomed everyone in his group. Mike was invited over one day by a group of kids in the cafeteria before lunch.

The kid, invigorated and anxious to meet new companions, starts bantering with the children, finding they are going to play hooky until the end of the day to go to a companion's home whose guardians are away.

The young man knew that skipping school was wrong, especially when we had a quiz scheduled. But he also longed fervently to make friends in his new environment. Guess what he did? He went with them without thinking of the consequences.

Now that's what peer pressure is. That I don't give a fuck attitude when your peers are up to something, you follow their lead even if it's wrong!

Just like Mike. Mike must have felt alone and aloof. I remember these words of Mike after I confronted him about why he missed such an important quiz, "I feel lonely and just want to make friends."

I get him completely, and so do you, right? Things do overwhelm us, especially loneliness. Students like Mike frequently give in to negative peer pressure due to feelings of loneliness and a desire for acceptance.

Negative Peer Pressure Deteriorates Your Well-Being!

Love, peer pressure that isn't kind can hurt your mental and emotional health. It can make you feel like a storm or like you don't know who you are. We'll examine how it affects your self-esteem, happiness, and confidence. The bright side is you can endure the storm and emerge stronger from it.

We can't move ahead without grasping the significance of setting boundaries that are healthy for you! Let's make the most out of our discussion on peer pressure and see how to establish boundaries to save your behind.

Setting Healthy Boundaries

Imagine this: You are at a party with lots of people, and it seems like everyone is trying to get you to do something that contradicts your values. As Ariana describes in her testimonial, she explains how setting a boundary helped her overcome peer pressure:

"When I was unaware of healthy boundaries, I used to battle peer pressure and frequently wound up doing things I felt awkward with just to fit in. Regardless, everything changed when I embraced the idea of defining solid boundaries. It gave me the certainty to express no to things that didn't line up with my qualities and convictions. Presently, I can oppose peer pressure without having a blameworthy or restless outlook on it.

Having sound boundaries permitted me to focus on my prosperity and spotlight the things that really make a difference. I can make decisions that are best for me, regardless of what other people think, because it's like wearing armor of self-respect and self-awareness. I'm grateful for the sense of freedom and authenticity that healthy boundaries have brought into my life. They have changed my life."

Do you know that your secret superpower is establishing an invisible boundary around you that secures you just like Ariana did? Yes, it surely is, making it a safe place for you to be yourself!

It's time to get into the world of setting healthy boundaries based on the testimonials of Ariana. Also, now that you know how to identify both positive and negative peer pressure.

It's like saying, "I know who I am, and I'm going to protect my authenticity and well-being!" while wearing stylish sunglasses.

Therefore, let's investigate what healthy boundaries are all about.

Gaining Insight Into "Boundaries"

Like personal fences, boundaries define and safeguard one's identity, values, and limits. You display these "no trespassing" signs to protect your individuality, well-being, and confidence. You can think of them as your superpower cape, allowing you to make decisions that are true to who you are. Ariana also wore this extraordinary cape of protection around her as she developed healthy boundaries.

Signs That Boundaries Are Healthy

So, how can you tell if you have established appropriate boundaries? Here are some warning signs to watch out for:

- **Know who you are:** In order to establish healthy boundaries, it is essential to comprehend who you are, what you stand for, and your values. It's similar to having a GPS that shows you the way.

- **Go with your gut:** Your instincts are similar to your inner compass. If something doesn't feel right or fails to line up with your qualities, believe that inclination. You know what's best for you from your gut.

- **Be able to say "no:"** It can be empowering to say "no." It's not about being rude or selfish; rather, it's about putting your well-being first and respecting your limits. Learn to be more assertive and to say "no" when something doesn't feel right.

- **Select the ideal friends:** You should be around people who respect and support your boundaries. While toxic friendships can weaken your boundaries, true friends will lift you and help you grow. Be picky about who you keep around.

- **Identify behaviors that are not acceptable:** Be on the lookout for actions that go against your boundaries or make you feel uneasy. Don't be afraid to speak up when you see someone going too far.

Essentials For Setting Boundaries

My girl, you must acquire essential phrases such as the ones I am going to mention in this section.

You might find yourself in situations where you are occasionally being pushed beyond your limits. You can help defuse those situations and maintain your composure by having a few key phrases at your disposal. A few examples include:

- "I appreciate your offer, but it doesn't feel right to me."

- "I require some time to consider it. Please allow me to respond."

- "I understand that you want me to join in, but right now, I have to put my own health first."

It's important to remember that these phrases empower you to assert yourself without escalating conflict. They will become your secret weapon against boundary-pushing individuals if you practice using them. You need to know when to put a full stop. Be well aware of your surroundings, and the gestures that deprive you of your peace!

Let's get a sense of how to deal with situations where you need to get your guard up by setting essential boundaries.

If It's Harmful, Let Go of It

You may encounter situations or relationships that are simply toxic and harmful to your well-being at times. Recognizing when something consistently violates your boundaries or is destructive is essential. In those instances, it is acceptable to distance yourself and let go. Your mental and emotional well-being ought to always come first.

Reciprocation is the key! When you expect people to respect your boundaries, you need to give their boundaries the same respect.

Respecting Others' Boundaries

Just as you want everyone to respect your boundaries, they must do the same. Recognize that everyone has values and limits. Avoid putting pressure on your peers to step outside their comfort zones and be mindful of those boundaries. Respecting and honoring the boundaries of others is an essential part of developing healthy relationships.

Here's My Journey Toward Self-development

Let me enlighten you with my teenage boundary-lacking personality and how I transformed into the kind of person I am now. I am sure it will inspire you!

I was once a people pleaser who lacked boundaries. I've always been a person who likes to help other people and is overly nice. I struggled to say no and frequently felt weighed down by commitments that didn't align with my true desires.

I was invited to a party by my classmates one day. To be honest, I didn't really want to go. I preferred to pursue my love of painting in my spare time because I had a tight schedule. However, I considered going due to the pressure to fit in and the fear of disappointing my friends.

My anxiety grew as the date for the party got closer. Deep down, I knew that attending the party would hurt my health and take time away from my true passion. It was a turning point in my ability to establish a healthy boundary.

Here's what I learned and applied through this self-development journey:

Prefer Open Conversation

I summoned the courage to have an open conversation with my friends with renewed determination. I said that while I was grateful for their invitation, I needed to give priority to my own well-being and creative endeavors. I feared their disappointment and judgment, so the conversation was difficult. But I knew it was more important to be true to myself.

You Deserve to Be Understood!

I was surprised by their understanding and respect for my decision, my friends. They were impressed by my capacity to advocate for myself and pursue my interests. In fact, they even supported my endeavors and encouraged me to continue exploring my artistic abilities.

The Ultimate Lesson

I learned the importance of setting boundaries that day. I realized it wasn't selfish to say no to things that didn't align with my values and passions; It was a self-care and self-respecting action. I regained control of my time, energy, and happiness by establishing healthy boundaries.

You're Already on the Ball!

I'm so happy for you! You are now well-versed in the process of establishing appropriate boundaries. Keep in mind that setting limits is the key to preserving your individuality, well-being, and confidence.

Don't hesitate to say "no" when necessary, trust your instincts, and embrace your individuality. Be surrounded by friends who encourage you and always respect their boundaries. It's time to set healthy limits and take control of your space!

Next, we'll take a look at assertiveness and decision-making abilities. Prepare to let loose your inner boss and make decisions that align with who you are. Stay tuned!

Strengthening Your Assertiveness and Decision-Making Skills

Trying to find your way through a maze without a map can often feel like navigating the turbulent waters of adolescence. There are a lot of choices and challenges during this time that can affect your future, Right, girl? Consequently, it is essential to cultivate strong assertiveness and decision-making abilities during this stage of life.

What Is It Like to Be Assertive?

Let's dive into it! Being assertive is like having a superpower that enables you to express yourself confidently, establish appropriate boundaries, and defend your beliefs.

Finding your voice and letting it be heard is the key, even in the face of opposition or peer pressure. You become the captain of your own ship when you develop assertiveness, steering it in a direction that is consistent with your values and goals.

Look at how beautifully assertiveness helps you express yourself now.

Assertive Self-Expression

Respecting other people's points of view and being open about your feelings, desires, and boundaries are all essential components of assertive self-expression. So, it's about finding the right balance between advocating for oneself and empathizing with your friends, expressing one's needs without undermining the rights or feelings of others.

Too Many Choices? Don't Worry, I've Got You!

The myriad of choices that life presents can make it easy to become overwhelmed when making decisions.

But do not panic, buddy, because I am here to provide you with a straightforward path to sound decision-making. So, buckle up, and let's get started!

Steps in Decision-Making

The following are some steps that will help you make decisions rather effectively and are critical for a better decision-making process! Here we go:

Step 1: Recognize the Issue

Think of yourself as a detective who solves problems, figuring out what's happening and what needs to be done.

Step 2: Collect Details

Imagine yourself as an experienced scholar seeking guidance from reliable sources. Reach out to your peers for advice and fresh perspectives without hesitation. It's like having a group of knowledgeable mentors by your side to support you!

Step 3: Find Out What You Value

Imagine you are an explorer who goes deep within your heart to discover what matters to you. During the decision-making process, your values will be your compass.

Step 4: Let's Do Some Brainstorming!

Take a pen and paper and let your creative juices flow. Make a list of all the options, no matter how crazy or unusual they may appear. It's like having an idea-sharing session with your closest friends, where you can come up with anything.

Step 5: Consider the Consequences

Imagine that you are an expert strategist evaluating each decision's possible outcomes. Consider both the positive and negative outcomes, like a professional gamer making strategic moves in a video game.

Step 6: Make Up Your Mind

My courageous decision-maker, rely on your instincts. Imagine yourself confidently selecting the best choice that satisfies your objectives and values. You can do this!

Step 7: Make a Strategy

Take on the role of an architect and create a blueprint for success. Create a strategy that will lead you to your desired outcome by breaking down your decision into steps that can be carried out.

Step 8: Make a Move

It's time to carry out your strategy! Imagine that you are a superhero in action, bravely executing the actions required to make your decision a reality.

Step 9: Learn and Reflect

Reflect on the outcomes as if you were a wise observer after taking action. Make the most of your newfound knowledge to help you make decisions in the future, learn from your failures, and celebrate your achievements.

I want you to know, my amazing girl, that you can choose your own path and act confidently. Take pride in your ability to make decisions and be assertive, and watch as you overcome any challenges you face!

Do you want to know what good you can achieve through making healthy decisions? Here we go!

Advantages of Effective Decision Making

You'll be able to handle the ups and downs of adolescence with greater self-assurance and resilience if you improve your decision-making and assertiveness skills.

Remember, you can control your destiny and steer your ship. Therefore, take pride in your assertiveness, make well-thought-out choices, and watch as you chart a course toward an authentic and satisfying life.

Lastly, it's time to use your self-advocacy skills and become your own greatest advocate.

Building Self-Advocacy Skills

We'll talk about what self-advocacy is, why it's important, and how it helps you build your confidence and self-esteem in this section. Get ready to own your power!

Defining Self-Advocacy

Self-advocacy is like being a cheerleader for yourself. It's about getting to know yourself, showing that you're confident in your skills and knowledge, and working on areas where you might be lacking. We will discuss the true meaning of self-advocacy and the reasons why it is a game-changer for resisting peer pressure.

Getting to Know Your Rights

Girl, it's time to understand your rights! We'll talk about how knowing your rights gives you the power to make educated choices, set boundaries, and shield yourself from bad influences. You will be equipped with the means to defend yourself because knowledge is power.

I have highlighted some major points in the upcoming section to guide you to understand your rights!

Participating and Speaking Up

Now, it's time to shine and get involved in activities and causes that reflect your values. We'll talk about how strong self-advocacy can be through speaking up, whether at school, in your community, or on social media. Your voice matters, and now is the ideal time to allow it to be heard.

Working Together and Asking For Help

Occasionally, you require a little assistance from your team. We'll talk about how important it is to work together with people who share your values and can help and encourage you.

When you need assistance, don't be afraid to ask for it. You can work together to resist peer pressure and bring about positive change.

Positive Self-Statements Go a Long Way

Imagine this: You are declaring, "I am my own advocate, and I have the power to shape my destiny!" while standing in front of a mirror and looking yourself square in the face.

Self-advocacy is essentially that. It involves defending oneself, expressing one's wants and needs, and actively shaping one's life. So, let's get started and find out how powerful self-advocacy is.

Essence of Self-Advocacy

Being your own champion and superhero on life's journey is the essence of self-advocacy. It means knowing your values, goals, strengths, and weaknesses and confidently expressing them to the world.

It all boils down to recognizing your individuality and using your voice to advocate for your values. But what is the significance of self-advocacy?

Significance of Self-Advocacy

Self-advocacy is, without a doubt, empowering. You regain your voice and take charge of your life when you become your own advocate.

You no longer allow other people to direct your actions or make your choices for you. Instead, you take charge of your own ship and steer it toward success, contentment, and happiness.

Stay Confident, Fear No One!

Self-advocacy also aids in the development of self-esteem and confidence. You show the world and, more importantly, yourself that you are worthy, deserving, and capable by asserting your needs and speaking up for yourself. Like flexing a muscle, it gets stronger the more you use it.

Additionally, your self-confidence and belief in your abilities increase with your self-advocacy muscle.

Strategies for Self-Advocacy

So, how can you become an expert at advocating for yourself? Let's look at some practical strategies and methods:

Learn About Yourself

Find out who you are, what you value, and what you want from life. Effective self-advocacy is built on this self-awareness.

Be Confident in Your Abilities and Knowledge

Trust that you have valuable insights and knowledge to share and believe in your abilities. Share your expertise with others and speak up with conviction.

Make Amends for Your Shortcomings

Accept that everyone has room for development and improvement. Accept them as opportunities for development rather than ignoring them. To fill in any gaps, look for mentors, resources, or additional education.

Discover Your Rights

Get to know your freedoms in different parts of life—training, work, medical services, and so on. You can confidently advocate for equitable treatment and access to opportunities when you are aware of your rights.

Socialize More

Get involved in things, groups, or causes that align with your interests and values. You can have a greater impact and be an advocate for positive change in your community or the world as a whole by getting involved.

Take Baby Steps

Start by practicing self-advocacy in smaller settings that are less intimidating. This could be expressing your preferences in everyday situations, advocating for your needs with friends and family, or voicing your opinions in group discussions.

Find a New Line of Work or Volunteer

Self-advocacy can be greatly improved through participation in volunteer or work-related activities. It lets you show off your skills and abilities, take on responsibilities, and assert yourself.

Never Be Afraid to Ask for Assistance

Recall that requesting help is an indication of solidarity, not a shortcoming. Don't be afraid to ask for help from friends, family, mentors, or professionals when you need it. Self-advocacy can't be done without it.

Collaborate With Others

Your journey toward self-advocacy will be supported and bolstered if you surround yourself with like-minded people. Work together to make your voices heard by joining forces with those who share your vision.

You become the hero of your story, writing a story that mirrors your fantasies, wants, and values. So, as you begin the remarkable self-advocacy journey, stand tall, speak up, and let the world hear your voice.

Journal Prompts

It's like having a conversation with yourself when you reflect on your experiences and points of view. Take out your journal, and let's get started with these provocative questions:

1. Think back on a time when you felt like you were being forced to do something you didn't want to do. What was the situation like? How

were you feeling at that time? Was there anything you could have done to avoid it?

2. Conceive a situation in which you successfully resist peer pressure. How would you make choices that align with your values and assertively communicate your boundaries?

3. Look for dependable friends or adults who can help you resist peer pressure. How can you approach them for advice and support?

Putting It All Together

To help you succeed in your battle against peer pressure, here are five important takeaways from this chapter:

- Be aware of the benefits and drawbacks of peer pressure.

- To safeguard your individuality and well-being, establish healthy boundaries.

- Stay true to who you are by improving your assertiveness and decision-making abilities.

- Recognize that self-advocacy is a potent strategy for boosting self-esteem and making your voice heard.

- Talk to adults and trusted friends who can help you handle peer pressure.

Key Takeaways

I'm so proud of you! You now know how to get through peer pressure's thrilling ups and downs. You will now step into a new journey of finding your authenticity in a digital world and its significance on your mind, body, and soul.

Prepare to experience some productive social presence instead of chasing clout. Learn how to become your best and most fabulous self. It will be like a day at the spa for you!

Therefore, buckle up and prepare for the subsequent excursion on our path to empowerment.

Chapter 6:

Unmasking Social Media: Finding Authenticity in a Digital World

Comparison is the thief of joy. –Theodore Roosevelt

Do you know what peculiar phenomenon has emerged in the era of pixels and screens? A world where authenticity and masks coexist!

Hey there, girl! Welcome to the realm of social media, where we find ourselves entangled in a delicate balance of self-expression, connection, and the hunt for validation and approvals. It's like a costume party where everyone wears the costume they want and looks perfect.

People carefully choose the only perfect parts of their lives to share. Behind those filters and perfectly posted pictures, there's a world that is far from reality.

But as we immerse ourselves in this digital realm, a question arises: How genuine are we truly in this virtual realm?

Let's answer this question in this chapter by unmasking social media. We're going to explore its curated nature and discover how we can navigate it with authenticity.

From there, we'll start our journey of establishing a healthy relationship with social media because, let's just accept it, we can't kick it out of our lives. However, we can flip the coin and see the other side of it, right?

So, get ready to dive deep into the digital world and learn how to live in this tapestry of social media. We'll address the perils of comparison and the negative impact it has on our mental health.

Also, we'll explore the strategies for developing self-awareness and mindfulness so that you can live in this world with your authenticity.

Let's dive into this!

Recognizing the Curated Nature of Social Media

Let's face it. Social media holds a greater significance in our lives, especially for us teenagers! It's where we find friends, connect with them, stay updated on trends, and seek validation. But, hey, beneath the surface lies a deceptive reality.

Social media platforms are designed to show the best and most positive aspects of people's lives! It's like entering a magical world where everything is just perfect! It's important to realize that social media doesn't always show the whole story.

Remember that what we see online is often a highlighted reel carefully chosen to showcase the best moments. Let's remove our rose-tinted glasses and see things from a whole new perspective (Tiggemann & Anderberg, 2019).

In a world where it's easy to get lost, there are stories that remind us of the power of authenticity and genuine connection. One such story is that of a teenage girl named Gray. She was a creative and determined teenager who started her own blog, Wondermint Kids, at the age of eight. She started with the intention to make friends and interact with people. Unexpectedly, Gray's blog captured the hearts of over 15OK followers. Amazing, right?

She started posting about her unique perspective on life as a young lady. She became a source of inspiration for other people who liked the same things she did, like art, music, fashion, and trying out new books, foods, and places to visit.

As she grew older, she realized that her voice genuinely impacted her audience more. She recognized that social media only shows the best part of people's lives. And guess what? Our brave Gray wanted to challenge this notice. She wanted to create a space where authenticity and real stories could thrive.

So, *Girl Folk* was born-a platform specially designed for girls! Gray shared her authentic self here and created a safe haven where teenage girls like you could connect, share their experiences, and inspire one another.

What sets *Girl Folk* apart from others is its meaningful content. Gray and her team of amazing teenage writers are dedicated to creating stories that delve deeper than just surface-level concerns. They cover a wide range of topics, including mental health, self-care, travel, cooking, and more, focusing on recognizing and overcoming the challenges that girls encounter in their daily lives.

One of the things that make *Girl Folk* really special is how collaborative it is! Gray and her team of teen writers are based on the beautiful and peaceful island of Orcas, but they love connecting with girls from all over the world! Collaborating virtually creates a welcoming environment for girls to connect and learn from each other's unique perspectives.

Gray's idea for *Girl Folk* has grown from her first blog to a non-profit organization that was run by girls for girls. It's amazing how being genuine to yourself can have such a positive impact, and it's so important to have places where people can freely express who they truly are.

As you discover the world of social media, let Gray's story inspire you. Let's embrace authenticity in a world that values only perfection. Together we can make this world a place where everyone's voice is appreciated and valued. Remember that behind the carefully edited posts and filtered photos are real people with unique stories and experiences to share. Let's aim to build meaningful connections online by being genuine to ourselves and showing our authentic selves.

When we acknowledge that social media is curated, we can feel more confident in our ability to see beyond what's presented on the surface.

Let's shift our focus from comparison to appreciation.

Understanding that each individual goes through ups and downs, challenges, and imperfections is important. It's crucial to remind the world that social media distorts the truth.

It's important to remember that everyone has their own struggles and insecurities; even those who post stunning photos or glamorous posts suffer from the thing we never know.

So, let's explore the digital world with a positive outlook and make our lives much easier.

Developing a Healthy Relationship With Social Media

Developing a healthy relationship with social media sounds like a tough job. But hey, listen up! Fostering positive habits and behavior for digital engagement is important in today's world, particularly concerning the impact of social media on our mental health.

Social media platforms offer convenience and connection, but accept it or not, these connections cannot fully replace real-world human interactions, right? Real-world interactions play a crucial role in alleviating stress, boosting happiness, and enhancing mental well-being.

Picture this: You meet your best friends on the weekend, share gossip and secrets, and have all the fun. How does it feel? Ask yourself? A kind of relief, right? Now suppose your best friend moved to another city or country.

You are connecting on the phone, making video calls, sharing memes on Instagram, and sharing everything. Now how does this feel? Something is missing, right? And when the urge to meet them isn't fulfilled, it leads to feelings of loneliness, anxiety, and depression.

Although online interactions on social media lack the psychological benefits that face-to-face interactions have, there are still positive aspects to consider. Just as in the above scenario, imagine not having any connection with your friend at all (Kruzan & Won, 2019).

Isn't it amazing how social media allows us to stay in touch with loved ones worldwide, make new friends, and discover new communities?

It's also a great platform for raising awareness about important causes, finding emotional support, and expressing our creativity. It can also be an excellent means to get knowledge and learn new things, especially for people who live in remote areas or have limited social independence.

Let's not forget about the negative experiences associated with social media, including feelings of inadequacy, fear of missing out (FOMO), social media addiction, anxiety, isolation, depression, cyberbullying, and self-absorption. Seeing manipulated images on social media can trigger insecurities and dissatisfaction.

FOMO can lead to anxiety and excessive use of social media. And when you excessively use social media, the feeling of loneliness increases. You start prioritizing online interactions over in-person relationships, which can become a reason for mood swings and, ultimately, mood disorders. Above all these issues, cyberbullying and self-centeredness prevailed so much that every other person is a victim of it!

Hey, pause for a moment. Too much negativity, right? Take a deep breath, then resume reading.

The point of telling you about the negative aspect for your awareness, my dear! Finding a balance between online and offline interactions is key to promoting positive digital engagement.

It's great to prioritize face-to-face connections and be mindful of the impact of social media on our mental health. By reducing excessive social media use and being aware of the curated content we consume, we can take important steps toward maintaining our mental well-being.

Great news! By adopting healthy habits and behaviors, individuals can consciously navigate social media and protect their emotional and psychological well-being. So, it is essential to re-evaluate your online habits and find a healthier balance.

Let's discuss some of the important habits that you can adopt for healthy social media use.

Healthy Habits for Social Media Use

Social media offers a variety of opportunities for connections and self-expression, and it's crucial to establish a healthy and positive relationship with it. Here are some of my secret tips that help me:

Turn On Your Social Media Privacy Settings

Okay, let's talk about how important it is to protect your personal information in this digital age. We all know we live in a world where everything can happen in just a few clicks. Social media is a great way to share your life with your friends and family, but it's crucial to take control of your online presence.

Think of your social media accounts as your personal kingdom, where you're the queen. By adjusting your account to private, you get to decide who to get a VIP pass to your kingdom. It's like a bouncer at the entrance that ensures only the right people get in.

Privacy settings can also do more than just control who sees your content. They can keep you safe from cyber threats and unwanted attention. By setting boundaries and limiting access to your personal information, you're taking control of your online presence and protecting yourself from potential threats (Baker, 2018).

So, if you want to keep your kingdom safe and secure and don't want anyone to peek into your life, then grab the phone and go to the privacy settings right now. Today's technology provides you with a variety of privacy options you can customize according to your preferences. It's time to take charge and rule your social kingdom like the fabulous goddess.

Schedule Time to Use Social Media and Plan Intervals to Step Away

Ah, social media-the land of endless scrolling, addictive content, and, ooh, how can we forget about these adorable cat videos that keep us distracted for hours? I've been there, my friend, falling down that addictive rabbit hole and losing track of time. It's like a toxic partner that doesn't let you leave. But, fear not because here is what I want to share with you that helps me, too: Setting boundaries that's the only way to maintain a healthy relationship with social media.

Think of social media as your favorite amusement park. You go there, enjoy the rides, savor the cotton candy, and capture memories, but you also make sure that you don't miss out on the other amazing things life has to offer.

So, here is the plan: let's schedule time for your social media usage. I'm not saying that you have to follow a rigid schedule like a robot. Of course, we can have cheat days too! Flexibility is the key here. Life is full of surprises, and it's okay to take some extra time to enjoy social media whenever you feel like it! Great job! Your goal is to find a balance that works for you. Social media can be a fun and connecting tool, so let's make it work in our favor!

There's more to look forward to! Remember to take breaks from social media too! It's just as important as scheduling time for it. Just like you take a break during a run, your mind and well-being also need time away from the digital world. Hey there! It's a great opportunity for you to shift your attention toward other areas of your life that make you happy, help you develop, and give you a sense of satisfaction.

Take advantage of these intervals to discover new hobbies, have heartwarming conversations with your loved ones, or just pause and enjoy the beauty of the world around you. Just a friendly reminder that life is full of amazing experiences beyond our screens! By taking intentional breaks from social media, you'll open yourself up to new opportunities for personal growth, self-reflection, and meaningful connections. So go ahead and take that break, and see what amazing things life has in store for you!

Here is the example schedule that you could follow:

Morning:

Wake up, start your day, and don't immediately check social media.

Give yourself the first 30 to 60 minutes to do things for yourself, like exercise, meditation, or reading.

Resist the urge to reach your cell phone; after breakfast, you can use the phone for 30 minutes.

School Time:

Keep your phone on silent or in your bag during school hours so it doesn't get in the way.

Use breaks like lunch or break to check your social media and answer messages.

Set a specific time limit for social media use during breaks, such as 15 to 20 minutes.

After School:

Set aside a certain amount of time for social media, like 30 minutes to an hour, shortly after school homework and chores are done.

Use this time to catch up with friends, engage in positive conversation, and share your life updates.

Use productive apps or website blockers to keep yourself away from endless scrolling or other time-wasting activities.

Evening:

As the evening approaches, set limits and eventually reduce time on social media.

Plan to do things that don't involve screens, like hobbies, reading, spending time with family or friends, or pursuing other interests.

Aim for at least an hour before bed without a screen. This will help you sleep better.

Weekends:

On the weekends, you can use social media more freely, but you should still set boundaries.

Schedule specific times throughout the day to disconnect from the internet, go outside, or spend time with loved ones.

Understand Your Purpose When Logging Into Social Media and Stick To It

The wonderful world of social media, where there are always new things to try and interesting things to read. But in a sea of likes, comments, and trendy hashtags, staying connected to your real goal is important.

Before you open that app on your phone, take a moment to ask yourself, "What am I doing here?" Are you signing in to stay in touch with friends and family, get ideas for your creative projects, get inspiration from your favorite influencers, or share your own unique voice with the world? Understanding why you go online each time is like having a map that helps you find your way through the vast world of social media.

Having a clear purpose is amazing! It can be a powerful anchor that keeps you grounded amidst the chaos of life. This way, you won't get lost in the tapestry of endless scrolling, mindless comparison, and time-wasting traps. You will be proud of yourself for remaining true to yourself and your values, even when there are so many tempting distractions out there. You'll rock like sunshine, trust me!

View Other People's Posts as an Inspiration Rather Than a Comparison

We all know when you see people living a perfect life-which is the only side of the coin that they decide to share, it's easy to get caught up in the comparison game, measuring our own worth against the highlight reels of others. But, let their life be your inspiration!

Let's not fall into the dangerous trap of comparison but instead use the power of perception. Wow, social media is such an amazing source of inspiration! It's like a virtual gallery filled with endless creativity, incredible achievements, and dreams that have become a reality. Let's turn things around and use other people's posts as a source of inspiration and motivation instead of letting envy or self-doubt get in the way of our own journey!

When you see a beautiful picture, an exciting story, or a big achievement shared by someone else, please take a moment to appreciate their work. Great job! Your success is a testament to your hard work, commitment, and skills. Keep up the good work. Let's join in their celebration and be reminded that amazing things can happen. Let their posts inspire you and awaken your own passions and desires. Remember, you have your unique journey, and it's not a race against anyone.

Think Before Posting

Remember the rush you feel to post something really exciting? It's so exhilarating to capture a moment, craft a catchy caption, and eagerly anticipate the reactions that flood our feeds, right? In the excitement of sharing our lives online, it's easy to overlook the consequences of our posts.

Here is the thing before hitting that "post" button, ask yourself: Does it align with my values? Will it be okay to post? Does it reflect the authentic, compassionate, and true-hearted self that I am? Will it hurt anyone?

Remember, my love, the digital world is an extension of who you're, so take advantage of the opportunity to radiate positivity and spread joy. Behind every screen, there's a human heart yearning for validation, approvals, and kindness. So, consider the potential impact of your post and your words, and spread love and kindness rather than negativity.

Now the choice is yours, whether you want to be remembered as someone who brings smiles, joy, and laughter to others or someone who can be a source of inspiration, enlightenment, and empowerment!

Remember: It's Not All Entirely True

Social media is sometimes a grand illusion into which we all can fall. As you scroll through your feed, those picture-perfect posts and flawlessly curated reels, always remind yourself that "It's not all entirely true." Promise me you'll say this to yourself next time you see any post that captures your heart, and you feel like, why don't I have it, okay? Because behind every post, there's an untold story, years of suffering, and things we can't even imagine sometimes.

So, whenever you find yourself mesmerized by someone's seemingly perfect life, take a step back and continually remind yourself that there's more to the story. Embrace the imperfect life, the unfiltered moments, and the vulnerability of being genuine to own yourself!

Fact-Check the Internet

In the coexisting world of masking and authenticity, it's essential to fact-check before believing and sharing the information. Not everything you see on social media is true. News and content are abundantly available at our fingertips, so it is crucial to check the credibility of sources. By fact-checking the news before sharing or even believing it, we can avoid being the ones who mislead others.

We should always remain vigilant against sensational language, exaggerated claims, and the absence of supporting evidence, as these are the biggest red flags for misinformation!

So, whenever you see something shocking, and you desperately want to share it with your friends, pause for a moment, fact-check it, and ask yourself if the information is reliable, and then hit the share button, okay?

Building a Positive Online Presence

Now that we've peeled back the deep layers of social media, it's time to explore the tips and tricks that will help you to build a positive online presence that reflects who you truly are. These will help you shape your digital footprint!

Digital footprint? Now what is it? Well, the digital footprint is the prints you leave due to your online presence. It includes the content you post, the comments you make, the interaction you've on the online platform, and the websites you visit (Mitchell, 2021).

Now back to our main focus—tips and secrets. Here they are:

- **Think about what you are posting:** Before posting anything online, it's crucial to think about what message you're conveying. Make sure it doesn't hurt anyone in any way. Think about the impact your post may have on others.

- **Proofread everything you post online:** The expression of your writing decides the impact of your message. Take a moment to proofread your posts, and ensure they are clear and well-written because it's all about presenting your best self!

- **Be Creative:** Let that creative side of yours shine through your online presence. Don't be afraid to share your talent, passion, and hobbies. Experiment with different formats by using the tech features of various social media apps. Embrace your unique style and share it with pride, of course, with only the right people.

- **Be Friendly on Social Media:** Social media? All about connection, my friend. Engage with other users, leave sweet and, of course, genuine comments, and support your friends. Spread the positivity like confetti. Make the social platform a welcoming and uplifting environment for everyone.

- **Be Authentic:** In a world where filters prevail, and facades dominate, authenticity is like a breath of fresh air. Don't be afraid to be your true self. Embrace your imperfections; share your vulnerabilities, only with the right ones, of course. Let your true personality shine through these online platforms. Remind yourself the most beautiful thing you can be is yourself!

Social Media Detox Challenge

Alright, time to do some social media detox! Are you up for the challenge? Take a break from social media. It will definitely have tremendous benefits for your mental well-being. Let it be just for two days. Let's disconnect from those likes, comments, and sharing.

Focus on yourself, use this time and reflect on your thoughts, engage in online activities, and rediscover the joys of the real world. I believe in you. You're strong. You can do this! Trust me; this is going to be a transformative experience!

Putting It All Together

1. Recognize the true nature of social media and develop a critical perspective.

2. Develop a healthy relationship with social media by setting boundaries and sticking to your true purpose.

3. View others' posts as inspiration rather than comparison.

4. Be mindful of your digital footprint and shape it positively.

5. Take a break from social media to recharge and prioritize your well-being.

Key Takeaways

So, we've unfolded the truth about social media and how it impacts our lives. By recognizing the reality of it and developing healthy habits, we can live authentically in this digital world!

Hey girl, our journey of self-admiration doesn't end here! In the next chapter, we'll explore the importance of recognizing stress triggers, developing coping skills, building resilience, and prioritizing self-care to navigate the challenges of teenage life with confidence!

Chapter 7:

Navigating Stress in

Teenage Life

Almost everything will work again if you unplug it for a few minutes… including you. –Anne Lamott

Welcome to Chapter 7 of our empowering journey, where we'll delve deeply into the crazy world of stress and learn how to deal with it like pros. Teenagehood can be like riding a wild roller coaster, right? However, don't worry!

Stress is like that unwelcome guest that shows up when it's least expected—ugh! In this chapter, we will look at some seriously awesome ways to identify stressors, learn effective coping mechanisms, build resilience, and prioritize self-care.

Prepare to master stress management and live a life of immense well-being and confidence. Let's absolutely carry this out!

Recognizing Stress Triggers

Teens can and will worry about anything. It is pointless to assign a cause to teenage stress.

Each of our lives unfolds uniquely, and there are experiences that we will not be able to share with others—or that we may not want to share in some cases.

I bet you want to know more about stress so you can navigate it better, right? Let's not waste time and dive into it!

How Do We Define Stress?

Stress prevails when people are under pressure, overwhelmed, or unable to cope with situations.

Positive Impact of Stress

Stress cannot always be bad, right? We can still benefit from a small amount of stress and be motivated to accomplish objectives like taking an exam or giving a speech.

An Excess of Everything Is Bad

Experiencing excessive stress, particularly when it feels out of hand, can negatively impact your relationships, as well as your physical and mental health, and even your mood.

However, when your body's stress response system begins to malfunction, the same feelings can become obstacles that prevent you from performing your best. According to research, several conditions can be sparked or exacerbated by stress, in addition to impeding the operation of various body systems (Yaribeygi et al., 2017).

It's critical to know the warning signs, right? Are you feeling completely exhausted, anxious, or overwhelmed? That is stress knocking on your door, indeed.

The Effect of Stress on Your Body

Bodily functions that take place without your conscious effort, like your heart rate, breathing, and other bodily functions, are all controlled by the autonomic nervous system. During stressful situations, stress causes the heart rate to rise, pupils to dilate, and other symptoms of the fight-or-flight response. This response can wear down the body and cause physical and emotional symptoms. Do you know that at least once a month, 51% of teenagers are told that they look or feel stressed? How worrisome!

Symptoms of Stress

Dear reader, make sure you notice the signs of stress to effectively deal with its negative impact on you! The following are some of the physical symptoms of stress (Pugle, 2021):

- muscle tension

- tension-type headaches

- body pain

- back pain

- chest pain

- the sensation that your heart is racing

- stomachaches

- pale or flushed skin

- headaches

- dizziness

- shortness of breath

- increased heart rate

- Increased blood pressure

- trouble sleeping

- digestive issues like bloating, diarrhea, or nausea

As we have now considered most of the symptoms of stress, we will now move toward exploring how these signs prevail in you.

Events Leading To Stress

Let's find out what the specific life events that lead to stress are:

Physical Changes and Whatnot!

A common trope in the story of life is that a teen's body is always changing, and these changes can be amazing or awfully awkward. You are experiencing a strange phase between childhood and adulthood in which your bodies develop irregularly, at irregular intervals, and with irregular focus, which is why it is a common occurrence.

Ingrain It in Your Minds!

Some teens mature earlier; some mature later. Unfortunately, teens, like children, can be extremely cruel to one another. Changes in your body are a common cause of stress and anxiety, resulting in issues with self-esteem that are already being propagated by your exposure to social media.

Seek Help From Elders

There is no simple solution to these problems. However, you need to concentrate on getting assistance from the older generation in becoming more at ease with who you are right now.

Social Stress

One of the most prevalent types of anxiety disorders is social anxiety. Do you know that the percentage of teens experiencing anxiety has skyrocketed to one-third of the population, and many of these cases involve social anxiety? Yes, bud. Isn't it alarming? A social anxiety disorder revolves around fear and worry of embarrassment, perceived self-image, gossip, or the preference for a small group of people and even solitude.

Teens who suffer from social anxiety disorders constantly worry about how they will be perceived and will go to great lengths to avoid situations where they might be required to meet new people. You definitely need to kick this habit!

Normalize Seeking Professional Help!

In some cases, therapy and anti-anxiety medication should be used professionally to treat social anxiety disorders. But keep in mind that self-medication is not recommended to be done; only prescribed medication should be taken to deal with stress.

Family Discord

I am aware that things can get ugly sometimes, even in your own home. It is another common source of stress. Our home environment can have both a tremendously positive and a tremendously negative impact on us.

This can be the case, whether it is due to a raucous family, younger siblings, crowded living areas, a lack of privacy, or more serious issues at home, such as substance abuse or parental conflicts.

In either case, dealing with issues at home is more difficult than it sounds. I am well-aware of it. Yet, these things can be fixed through family therapy.

Family Therapy Can Help

In certain situations, family therapy can address domestic issues during treatment. This is an illustration of group therapy, in which a therapist collaborates with the patient and multiple family members to help them reconcile, gain a deeper understanding of one another, or learn how to provide more effective support.

Poor Sleep

How you treat your body greatly influences your mental health, including anxiety. A difference of even half an hour per day can significantly impact your memory, cognitive abilities, mood management, and ability to think calmly.

So, now you know why you remain stressed for longer when you have had countless sleepless nights.

Missing a party or a sleepover with friends is okay. Get yourself enough time to sleep, at least!

Better Sleep, Better Life

Your mental health can benefit greatly from better sleep routine practices like creating a cool, dark space before going to bed, avoiding screens an hour before bed, and engaging in more physical activity throughout the day.

Traumatic Events

Your stress levels can be impacted long-term by traumatic events like the death of a friend or family member, accidents, illness, or being subjected to emotional or physical abuse. It's also important to notice that approximately 10% of teens experience dating violence.

Significant Life Changes

Like adults, teens experience stress as a result of significant life transitions. You can experience stress as a result of things like starting a new school, moving, and changes in the family's composition (such as divorce). I understand that not knowing how to adapt to major changes is overpowering and can be troublesome for my girl.

Academic Stress

It is notable that you may experience a lot of stress related to school, from grades to test scores to college applications. Many of you worry about keeping up with your classmates, pleasing teachers and parents, and meeting academic requirements.

Academic stress can also be exacerbated by having insufficient time management skills or feeling overwhelmed by the amount of work. So, take a deep breath and keep striving to grow effectively (Heckman, 2017).

Now that we know what causes our stress, let's learn some amazing coping strategies. We'll be able to control our stress and keep our cool even when things get crazy with these babies. Therefore, prepare to add some serious superhero moves to your arsenal of stress-reducing techniques!

Coping Skills for Stressful Situations

Take it one day at a time, do not get too stressed out!

We get overwhelmed by stress, but it's a part of life, love. It's time we unleash that hidden self that knows how to manage all the stress and keep ourselves in a perfect balance. So, coping mechanisms are really important not to let things hurt you in the long run!

Steps for Healthy Coping

The following steps and skills can be used to deal with any situation that stresses you out. Take the time to understand the circumstance, maintain a positive outlook, act, and make any necessary adjustments. Stress won't stand a chance if you have these skills on hand!

Step 1: Understanding the Circumstances

Okay, the first step when stress strikes is to comprehend the circumstance. Getting to the bottom of the matter is like donning a cool pair of detective glasses. Assess the stressor momentarily and inquire, "What's really happening here?" We can gain clarity and control when we understand the situation. To know what distresses you, you can write it down in your journal.

For Example:

Consider this: Emma is panicking because the big game is coming up. She's thinking a million different things, like, "What if I mess up? What if we fall short?" However, Emma takes a deep breath and reaffirms her understanding of the circumstance. She realizes that being anxious prior to a game is normal and does not guarantee failure.

Emma confidently takes the field and prepares to give it her all with this new perspective. And what's more? As her team prevails in the game, Emma discovers that understanding the situation can transform her stress into victory.

Step 2: Commit to a Positive Attitude

Okay, lovely people, let's talk about attitude's power. It's easy to let negativity take over when stress knocks us down. But that gloomy life is not what we're about! Even when we're under a lot of stress, we can choose to keep a positive attitude. It's like turning on the "Ugh, this is the worst!" switch to "I'm capable of handling anything!" Remove the negative energy from yourself and cultivate gratitude to maximize positive thinking.

For Example:

My buddy Jake is the king of positivity. Let's meet him. He reminds himself to keep a positive attitude whenever he encounters a stressful situation. Therefore, rather than dwelling on his nerves when he has to give a presentation in front of the entire class, he pumps himself up with thoughts like, "I've prepared for this, and I'm going to rock it!"

In addition to helping him deliver an outstanding presentation, Jake was extremely grateful to even appear on the stage and present. Because of his upbeat outlook, whenever he stumbled over a word, he would remind himself that he should be grateful for the opportunity and capability to share his knowledge with others.

You ought to act like Jake to prioritize your inner positivity-filled goddess!

Step 3: Take Action

So, my terrific warrior, it's time to act and demonstrate to stress who is in charge. It's like saying, "I'm not going to let stress get the best of me!" as we don our superhero capes. Gather your strength, take a deep breath, and confront the stress head-on.

The most important thing is to act, whether that means organizing your work into manageable chunks, asking for help from family and friends, or practicing relaxation techniques as a self-care regime.

For Example:

Let's discuss Mia now. She was my favorite junior through high school. Having an extensive to-do list used to make her feel overwhelmed. However, Mia made the decision to act. She tackled each of her tasks one at a time, breaking them up into smaller, more manageable chunks.

She also sought assistance from her friends and took breaks to practice yoga and meditate. Mia turned her stress into a force for good by acting, and when she thought about how she used to let stress control her, she laughed.

What have you learned from this? Put this into practice and get the best of the stress.

What Things Can You Change

Here's the deal: It's okay that we can't control everything. However, realizing that there are things we can alter gives us power. Whenever you feel stressed out, ask yourself, "What can I do to change the situation?" We feel more confident and less stressed when we take charge of the things we can change.

You Can Definitely Win Anything!

My cousin Alex is the master of adaptability, trust me on this! Alex focuses on making as many changes as possible when confronted with a stressful circumstance. Like the time their group project appeared to be a complete failure, Alex took charge rather than becoming anxious.

They coordinated a study session, communicated with their teammates, and even devised a novel solution to a problem. Alex turned a potential stress bomb into a high-five moment by changing what they could. Congratulations, Alex!

Do you want to know about the techniques that promote relaxation in you? Let's find out.

Relaxation and Mindfulness Techniques

Finding moments of zen in the midst of stress can be life-changing, ladies. You can find peace in the chaotic world by practicing mindfulness and relaxation techniques like deep breathing exercises, meditation, and even yoga. These wonderful strategies not only help you deal with stress but also improve your well-being as a whole. Totally fun, isn't it?

We need to have a healthy means of discharging stress when it strikes, right? Find things to do that make you happy and help you relax. Do whatever makes you feel great, whether it's playing the guitar, creating masterpieces, writing in a journal, or going for a run. It is important to remember that taking care of yourself is not selfish at all!

When it comes to coping with stress, you've got what it takes to cope like champions! In the upcoming section, we will demonstrate to the world our resilience and level it up.

Developing Resilience

We're not going to let major setbacks in life discourage us, ladies. Let's change our perspective and see challenges as opportunities for growth rather than obstacles. Resilience is the ability to overcome challenges with greater strength. Never lose sight of the fact that you can conquer anything!

Definition of Resilience

Resilience, according to psychologists, is the process of successfully adapting in the face of adversity, trauma, tragedy, threats, or significant sources of stress, such as family and relationship issues, serious health issues, workplace and financial stressors. However, resilience includes "returning quickly" from these troublesome encounters. And the best part is it leads to self-improvement (American Psychological Association, 2012).

It's necessary to have a thorough understanding of the traits of a resilient person so my super girls can cultivate them effectively in their personality, right? Keep reading my beautiful reader!

Traits of a Resilient Person

People who are resilient typically possess a number of distinct traits that assist them in overcoming obstacles in life. The following are some indications of resilience:

A Survival Mindset

People who are resilient consider themselves to be survivors. Regardless of the difficulty, these survivors are aware that they can persevere until they are successful.

Regulating Your Emotions Effectively

However, this does not imply that resilient individuals do not experience strong emotions such as rage, sadness, or fear. Resilience is defined as the capacity to control one's emotions in the face of stress. It indicates that they are aware that those emotions are fleeting and can be controlled until they pass.

An Unmatched Sense of Control

People who are resilient typically have a strong internal focus on control and the belief that their actions can influence the course of events.

Skills For Solving Problems

When problems arise, resilient people try to find solutions that will make a difference by looking at the situation logically.

Self-Compassion

Self-compassion and acceptance of oneself are additional indicators of resilience. When things are hard, resilient people treat themselves with kindness.

Social Assistance

Another sign of resilience is having a strong network of people who are there to help you. People who are resilient are aware of the significance of having support when they require assistance.

Types of Resilience

The following are some types of resilience:

Physical Resilience

The body's ability to adapt to change and recover from physical demands, illnesses, and injuries are all examples of physical resilience.

Mental Resilience

A person's capacity to adapt to change and uncertainty is known as mental resilience. When faced with adversity, resilient types are adaptable and composed.

Emotional Resilience

Being able to control one's emotions in stressful situations is an essential part of emotional resilience. Resilient individuals tend to be in touch with their inner life and are aware of their emotional responses.

Social Resilience

The capacity of groups to recover from challenging circumstances is referred to as social resilience or community resilience. It involves people coming into contact with others and working together to resolve issues that affect both individuals and groups (Cherry, 2022).

Here's How to Build Resilience

Keep these key-points in mind for cultivating a more resilient self, my dear!

Accept Positive Thoughts

My amazing friends, resilience starts with our thoughts. Accept positive thoughts that inspire you and give you power. Positive affirmations should take the place of self-doubt. Remind yourself of your strengths, achievements, and the fact that you are able to overcome any obstacle.

Reframe Negative Thoughts

It's time to put on our mental ninja masks and reframe any negative thoughts that come to mind. Find new perspectives and challenge negative beliefs. Find the positive aspects and growth opportunities in challenging circumstances. We can strengthen our resilience and maintain a positive outlook by reframing our negative thoughts.

Confront Your Fears

Brave warriors, I have a secret for you: When we face our fears head-on, resilience flourishes. Face the things that scare you and step outside of your comfort zone. Watch as your confidence grows as you take baby steps toward your fears. Keep in mind that courage is the willingness to face fear, not the absence of it.

Seek Assistance

We are all in this together. Seek assistance from people who inspire you and have faith in you. Reach out to trusted friends, family members, or a mentor for advice and support. Surround yourself with positive people who will encourage you during trying times.

Focus on Things Within Your Control

Resilience is focusing on what we can control. Concentrate on the aspects you can influence rather than dwelling on those outside of our control. You will feel empowered and ready to take action if you shift your focus.

Let me introduce you to Ethan who is a pro at concentrating on what is within his control. When faced with a challenging school assignment, Ethan focused on his own effort and preparation rather than worrying about external factors.

He made a study schedule, asked his classmates for help, and gave the project his all. Ethan turned a potentially overwhelming situation into a major success by concentrating on what he could control. Ethan, you can do this!

Find Meaning

Unlocking a buried superpower within yourself is the same as discovering your purpose. Take part in things that give you pleasure and line up with your qualities. Find a sense of purpose and meaning in your activities. When you have a clear sense of purpose, it becomes a light that guides you through difficult times and helps you be resilient and determined.

I want you to keep in mind that it takes time and practice to build resilience. You'll be able to conquer the obstacles of adolescence like a superhero armed with these powerful tools!

Next, we'll take a deeper dive into self-care, exploring how it can become our ultimate stress-fighting weapon. Prepare to deal with yourself like the celebrity you genuinely are!

Prioritizing Self-Care

Make time for yourself, sister, despite the frantic pace of school and responsibilities. Take some time off and recharge your batteries.

You can reflect on yourself, indulge in your interests, hang out with your ride-or-die team, or simply take some time to yourself.

Take care of yourself because it's like your secret weapon against stress. Let's get to know more about the benefits of self-care:

It's Not Selfish to Put Yourself First

Self-care is not selfish love. Taking care of yourself is like recharging your superpowers, giving you the mental and physical stamina to face any challenge so that you can shine brighter than ever before. It's all about feeding your mind, body, and spirit.

Learning to Have a Growth Mindset

Girl, when stress tries to change your mood, it's time to adopt a growth mindset. Believe that hard work and dedication can improve your intelligence and abilities. With this mindset, you will be able to face challenges head-on, gain knowledge from failure, and keep growing. Remember, you are in charge of your own success story.

Establishing Boundaries

Learning to say "no" and establishing appropriate boundaries is absolutely necessary. It is perfectly acceptable to prioritize yourself and decline activities that deplete your energy or cause you unnecessary stress.

Embrace the fact that you are in charge of your own life, and you ought to make a place where you can be happy and secure.

Now, let's examine how we can practice self-care in everyday life. Are you ready to include such positive habits in your life? Let's find out!

Ways to Self-Care

Impressive beauties, here I have mentioned some ways to practice self-care:

Get Some Beauty Sleep

Your well-being is enhanced by sleep. To refuel and rejuvenate, make getting a good night's sleep a priority. Dim the lights, establish a relaxing bedtime routine, and give yourself the gift of sound sleep.

Write in a Journal

Writing down your thoughts can be very therapeutic. Take a journal with you and let your feelings flow. Write about your hopes, fears, and achievements. You can freely express yourself and gain valuable insights into your own journey by keeping a journal.

Creative Expression

Imaginative darlings, let out your inner artist! Dance, play an instrument, paint, write poetry, or paint. You can express yourself authentically and find joy in the process of engaging in creative activities.

Practice Meditation

Find your zen for a moment. Meditation is similar to a mind-calming balm. Close your eyes, find a quiet place, and concentrate on your breathing. Through the power of mindfulness, you can let go of stress and find inner peace.

Try Doing Yoga

Yoga is a great way to find inner balance and practice poses. Strength, flexibility, and inner calm can be developed through this ancient practice that incorporates mindfulness, movement, and breath. Set out on a journey of self-discovery by rolling out your mat.

Take a Shower

Relax in a soothing, warm bath and let your worries go. Play soft music and put on some calming scents for a moment of pure relaxation. Treat yourself like a king or queen!

Exercise

Active warriors, get moving and let those endorphins out! Dance, running, or playing a sport are all great activities to take part in. Not only does exercise improve your physical health, but it also improves your mood and relieves stress.

Apply Nail Polish

Do-it-yourself-manicures are a great way to indulge yourself. Make your favorite nail polish colors your own, experiment with designs, and let your fashionista side shine through. It all boils down to embracing your individual style!

Gardening

Maintain your green thumb and connect with the natural world. Grow your own vegetables and herbs or plant some flowers. Gardening allows you to slow down, appreciate nature's beauty, and cultivate life for peace.

Take a Walk

Take a break from the hustle and bustle of everyday life by embarking on an outdoor adventure. Put on your hiking boots, get in some fresh air, and enjoy the splendor of the natural world.

Embrace Nature

Take a moment to appreciate the beauty all around you. Take note of the dazzling hues of a sunset, the chirping of birds, or the gentle touch of a breeze. Interfacing with nature can bring a feeling of quiet and help you to remember the marvels that encompass you.

Play with a Pet

Our days are brightened in a unique way by our furry friends. Spend time with your beloved pet or help out at a shelter by volunteering. An animal's joy and unwavering love can be a powerful comfort and happiness source.

Write a Letter to Yourself in the Future

Write a letter to the amazing person you will become in the future, and let your imagination soar. Think about your goals, aspirations, and dreams. Remind yourself of your incredible potential and share your hopes.

Meet New Friends and Talk to Them

Social associations are fundamental for your prosperity. Gather with friends, converse deeply, and laugh together. Be surrounded by positive people who can uplift you and make your heart sing.

Volunteer

Contribute to your community and improve the lives of people around you. You can help those in need, volunteer at a local charity, or support a cause you care about. At the point when you expand generosity, you influence others as well as develop a feeling of direction inside yourself.

Let's move ahead by including some positive affirmations to reduce stress in life.

Positive Affirmations for Stress

Let's now examine the power of positive affirmations, my amazing friends. These simple mantras have the potential to transform your stress management and confidence levels. With conviction, repeat them, and watch the magic happen:

- "I'll be fine."

- "I take in the good and let go of the bad."

- "I'm up for trying new and exciting things."

- "Thoughts can be changed; it is just a thought."

- "I contribute actively to my healing."

Putting It All Together

- Make self-care a top priority because it is so important to your health.

- Engage in activities that encourage physical activity, creativity, and relaxation.

- Nurture your soul by connecting with nature and appreciating its beauty.

- Develop social associations and encircle yourself with positive impacts.

- Utilize the power of affirmations that are positive to reduce stress and boost confidence.

Key Takeaways

Okay, awesome girls, you now know some seriously awesome ways to deal with stress in adolescence. You will overcome stress by identifying stressors, learning powerful coping strategies, strengthening your resilience, and making self-care a must.

Take the challenges as opportunities to laugh at yourself, and never forget how amazing you are. So, keep crushing that stress and rock on! You can do this!

As we come to the end of this chapter, keep in mind that self-care is your best tool for navigating the turbulent and stressful waters of adolescence.

Next, we'll look at personal development and how you can embrace the "firsts" of your life that can open up a world of possibilities in the following chapter. Prepare to embrace your inner butterfly and spread your wings to the fullest!

Chapter 8:

Embracing and Learning

from "Firsts" in Life

A mind that is stretched by a new experience can never go back to its old dimensions. –Oliver Wendell Holmes

Hey girls, welcome back to another exciting yet final chapter of our journey! Here we are going to unleash your inner adventures and conquer uncharted territories. This chapter will make you feel like you're on a rollercoaster ride taking you back to all those first experiences you ever had in your life.

Let me tell you about my first-ever solo dance performance back when I was in school. I was all set to embark on my performance; the spotlight was on me, the music started, and, wait for it, I tripped over my own feet and did a magnificent faceplant on the stage.

Cue the laughter! I was embarrassed, but I started laughing along with them, too. And trust me, those hilarious mishaps and unexpected twists are what make "firsts" worth remembering.

So, are you ready to embrace the oopsies, the blunders, and the awkward moments? Because, life is too short to take it seriously because it's never about avoiding failure but rather how we bounce back from it.?

Gaining the confidence to tackle those nerve-wracking yet hilarious "firsts" is like flexing a muscle. You start small, and with each unexpected detour, you grow stronger and become more resilient. It's all about how you embrace the journey and find a way to laugh at the mishaps along the way.

First, early baking experiences are mostly like a science experiment that has gone wrong. I baked my first-ever cake when I was in high school. I put on my apron; the world's best recipe was in my hand, and I was eagerly waiting for the mouthwatering masterpiece which I was ready to bake. But, oh, my innocent self forgot that baking can sometimes be a magical recipe for chaos.

As I poured the flour into the bowl, it ended up covering not just my counter but also my face, and in a minute, I turned into a bona fide flour monster. And when this monster tasted her creation, well, it was like I was eating stone! But hey, that's the beauty of baking.

You start from scratch and learn thousands of recipes that you shouldn't ever use again for baking, hehe! These experiences eventually lead you to be the smartest baker in the whole family, right? Well, that's where I am right now.

Today we're going to embrace the hilarious side of "firsts "and find the courage to explore something new, even if it involves stepping out of our comfort zones.

It's about developing the spirit of self-acceptance and allowing ourselves the freedom to make mistakes and create memories that we can look back on and either laugh at or be proud of.

Hey there, my amazing trendsetter! Are you ready to conquer your "firsts?" Whether it's your first kiss, first date, first dance, first-time joining a new club, or trying out a bold fashion trend, just remember that perfection is totally overrated. Let's embrace our imperfections and have some fun along the way!

Hey, you know what's awesome? Imperfections and unexpected twists and turns! They're what make our experiences truly remarkable and unforgettable. So, let's embrace the unexpected and enjoy the ride!

No worries if things don't go exactly as planned! Sometimes life throws us curveballs, but that just means we get to practice our swing. Plus, who wants a predictable life anyway? Where's the fun in that? Embrace the unexpected and see where it takes you! Don't worry if you trip, slip, or create a masterpiece of chaos every now and then. It's all part of the adventure, so it's okay to mess up!

Do you know what's great about messy moments? They always make for the best stories to share with your buds! And let's be real, those fits of laughter that come with them are the glue that keeps friendships together. So, embrace the mess and get ready for some serious belly laughs!

Let's jump into these "firsts" with a big smile and a positive attitude. Remind yourself that you're gaining some awesome life skills, building up your resilience, and discovering more about yourself. You are a brave soul! Every step you take toward your goals is worth celebrating, even if it leads to some funny mishaps along the way.

Keep taking those bold steps, and don't be afraid to laugh at yourself when things don't go as planned. You got this! Life is an exciting journey full of surprises and opportunities. Every time you try something new, you're getting closer to unleashing your inner superhero! So go ahead and conquer those "first" with confidence because you're destined for greatness. Let's show the world what you're made of! Don't sweat the small stuff—embrace the messiness and learn from those hiccups along the way. Life is a wild ride, so buckle up and enjoy it to the fullest!

Preparing for New Experiences

Let me impart some wisdom to you: embracing new experiences is like opening a treasure chest of personal development and self-discovery (Larson, 2009). It's stepping out of your comfort zone and diving straight into a world full of opportunities. Every new experience is a chance to spread your wings, explore new horizons, and unleash the hidden talents you never knew you had.

Let's think of it this way: Life is like a notebook, and every new experience is a chapter waiting to be written. How cool is that? By embracing these opportunities, your story gets a whole lot more colorful, exciting, and full of unforgettable characters. Trying new things can be scary, but it can also be super exciting!

Don't worry. We've all been there! It's totally normal to feel a little nervous when trying something new. Sure, it can be a bit nerve-wracking to step into the unknown, but think of all the amazing discoveries you could make! Plus, who knows what kind of fun surprises are waiting for you out there? I know it might seem scary, but trust me, the real magic happens when we step out of our comfort zones. Let's take a leap of faith together and see where it takes us!

Hey, you've got this! Embrace those new experiences with open arms and get ready for some exciting adventures. Don't be afraid to step out of your comfort zone. Take a deep breath, feel the power within, and jump right in like a boss!

When things get tough, just remember that those are the moments that will help you discover your inner strength and unleash your full potential.

So, let's embrace the challenges and enjoy the ride! Who knows, maybe we'll even learn some cool sailing tricks along the way. Remind yourself that there's no limit to what you can achieve!

Every new experience is like adding another shiny diamond to your personal growth crown. Keep shining bright! The world is waiting for you to conquer it with all your awesomeness! Let's go get 'em!

Here are some of the practical tips and strategies that will help you navigate unfamiliar situations:

Understand Your Comfort Zone

Imagine that you are a young person who has never been brave enough to venture outside of your comfort zone. You don't like trying new things or taking risks, so you stick to familiar routines. One day you get an invitation from your friends to go on a mountain hiking trip with them. You are terrified of hiking because it is completely out of your comfort zone but accept her invitation and try to suppress the feeling of dread toward the unexplored world. You replace your anxiousness with a sense of exploration to go beyond your limits to attain pure bliss!

After careful consideration, you make the decision to take advantage of the opportunity. You assemble your boldness, put on your climbing gear, and leave on the excursion with your companions. As you begin climbing, you feel a combination of stress and energy. You push yourself beyond your usual limits with each step.

All through the hike, you explore new territories, unexpected barriers, and doubtful moments. However, you also get to enjoy breathtaking views, a sense of accomplishment, and your friends' support. As you arrive at the highest point and take in the glorious view, understand the magnificence that lies past your comfort zone. You say to yourself that "I am grateful that I came and got to experience such beauty of nature!"

You will learn the value of knowing your comfort zone and pushing it to its limits from this experience. It shows you that development, self-revelation, and essential encounters happen when you embrace unfamiliar experiences. Expand your horizons, discover new strengths, and build resilience by stepping outside your comfort zone.

Listen up! Understanding your comfort zone is like mapping out the cozy boundaries of your favorite hangout place. It's where you feel safe, secure, and comfortable.

But, the thing is, growth doesn't happen in the land of comfort. The moment you step out of your comfort zone, the magic starts happening (Stone & Stone, 2011).

Let's take a moment to reflect on the exciting possibilities that await you just beyond the boundaries of your comfort zone. What kind of things, activities, situations, or experiences make you feel at ease?

And on the flip side, what are some of the things that make you a little jittery, a tad nervous, but also excited? These are the indicators that you're teetering on the edge of your comfort zone.

So, resilient one, accept the discomfort! Step outside of your comfort zone and try something new. If you need to, take small steps. Take baby steps if you need to. Dip your toes into new experiences, and your zone will gradually expand.

And the best part is that the moment you step out of your comfort zone, it becomes larger. What used to scare and overwhelm you will eventually become your new normal.

Set Attainable Goals

When it comes to embracing new experiences, it's essential to break them down into smaller, attainable goals. Think of it like putting together a puzzle. Each small goal you set is like a puzzle piece that gets you closer to finishing the whole picture.

So, take a minute to think about the new experience you're about to embark on. What are specific goals you need to reach to be successful? Break them up into small pieces that you can handle one at a time. By doing this, you not only make the journey more manageable but also build up your confidence along the way.

Don't forget, Rome wasn't built in a day, and neither are great accomplishments. Set yourself up for success by setting attainable and realistic goals. They should be stretchable enough to push you out of your comfort zone but not so much that they become overwhelming.

Remember: No One Is Good at Anything at First

No one is immediately good at anything. We all start out as newbies, stumbling through things we are unfamiliar with. So, if you feel a little nervous or make a few mistakes when you try something new, know that you're not alone. All of this is part of the journey.

Accepting that you won't be great right away is a key part of your personal growth and development. It allows you to let go of the pressure to be perfect and put your attention on learning and getting better.

Remember, even the most successful people had to start somewhere, and they've also made mistakes along the way. Be kind to yourself and rock your first experiences like a pro.

Let me enlighten you with the story of a well-known personality. Maya Angelou, a famous black writer and civil rights activist, is an inspiring example of dealing with difficulty and committing errors along the way to progress in her writing career and even her personal life.

In spite of experiencing childhood in a racially isolated society and confronting poverty and inequality, Maya never let her conditions characterize her.

She pursued her passions and became an advocate for equality with resilience, determination, and a strong belief in herself. In her memoir *I Know Why the Caged Bird Sings*, Maya not only shared her own experiences, but she also inspired other people to face their own challenges and find their voices.

The story of Maya Angelou's life serves as a lesson to us about the power of overcoming obstacles and accepting one's own identity.

Claim Your Sphere of Control

Remember that you, and only you, have power over your actions and decisions when it comes to embracing new experiences. Don't waste your time worrying about things beyond your control; instead, focus on claiming your sphere of control. This means taking ownership of your own preparations and refocusing your efforts where they will have the most impact. This means shifting your energy toward the fact that you can influence and take charge of your own plans (Anyiam, 2022).

Instead of spending time and energy worrying about what might happen or how things will turn out, try focusing on getting prepared as best you can. By claiming your sphere of control, you empower yourself to take charge of your own journey. Remember, you may not have control over everything that happens, but you do have control over how you deal with it, right?

Give it your all, focus on what you can do, and trust yourself to deal with whatever comes your way with grace and determination.

Separate Yourself From the Experience

Mark my words: The outcomes of first-time experiences do not define your worth as a person. Don't let the outcome affect how you feel about yourself. Instead, pay attention to the experience itself.

Take it as a chance to grow, learn, and find out more about yourself. Think of it as an opportunity to push yourself, get out of your comfort zone, and learn new things. When you separate yourself from the experience, you free yourself from the weight of expectations and allow yourself to appreciate the journey to its fullest.

Approach an experience with curiosity and open-mindedness. Learn from both the things that go well and the things that go wrong because you know that they are all part of the process.

Remember, the real value is in what you learn, how much you grow, and the memories you make along the way.

So, stop worrying about how things will turn out and enjoy the beautiful messiness of the experience itself instead.

Celebrate Growth

Every step toward embracing new experiences is a reason to celebrate. Celebrate every little win and every big accomplishment because progress is progress, no matter how small. Give yourself a pat on the back for taking that leap of faith. Who knows what exciting opportunities and experiences await you now? Keep on being brave and bold!

Give yourself a round of applause for your bravery and determination every time you step out of your comfort zone! Congrats on your growth!

By celebrating your progress, you're not only boosting your confidence but also setting yourself up for success in future first-time experiences.

Reflect on Your Own Journey

Just a friendly reminder that your journey is completely unique and special, just like you! No one else can walk in your shoes or live your life, so embrace your individuality.

It's totally normal to feel like you're falling behind sometimes, but don't worry—you're right where you need to be! Focus on improving yourself and appreciating the beauty of your own road.

Comparing yourself to others can be a real buzzkill, so why not focus on your own journey instead? Trust me. You'll be amazed at how much progress you can make.

Look at you! You've come such a long way, and so many valuable lessons are waiting for you. So, let your strengths, abilities, and talents lead you to welcome new first-time adventures with a wide smile.

Embracing your own journey allows you to fully appreciate and value your growth and accomplishments as well.

Connect With the Community

The best way to tackle first-time experiences is to connect with a community of supportive people. Join a group of awesome people who have gone through similar experiences as you.

Find a supportive community that will lift you up and make you feel like you're not alone. Connect with positive, motivating individuals.

Find yourself a group of experienced individuals who can share their wisdom, give you a boost of confidence, and make you laugh along the way. Share your stories, fears, and successes with them.

Engaging with a supportive network not only enhances your self-assurance but also provides opportunities for interaction, learning, and expanding your zone.

Embracing Vulnerability and Taking Risks

Vulnerability means letting ourselves be honest, open, and susceptible, both emotionally and mentally. It's about accepting our true selves, including our fears, doubts, and flaws, and letting friends and family know about them.

Vulnerability is the desire to step outside of our comfort zones, take risks, and show up as our true selves, even when it feels uncomfortable or unsure (Adrian et al., 2019).

When we let ourselves be vulnerable, we open the door to deep self-discovery, emotional growth, and meaningful bonds with other people. When we let ourselves be seen, we can learn the most about ourselves, our wants, and our limits. It gives us a chance to face our fears, question what we think we know, and try out new things.

Vulnerability Leads to Success and Self-Growth

Allow me to tell you about my companion, Shae, who showed me the genuine force of vulnerability and risk-taking. She had consistently longed to begin her own online business; however, self-doubt and dread held her back for a very long time. She decided one day that she would now take a step to fulfill her goal. So brave of her, no? She presented her business concept to a group of potential investors with a shaky voice and trembling hands. She bared her soul and authentically shared her passion and vision in a nerve-wracking moment.

The overwhelmingly positive response surprised her. Not only did Shae get the money she needed, but the other people in the room were inspired by her bravery and vulnerability. They appreciated her valiance and respected her for facing the challenge. From that day on, Shae's business prospered, and she turned into a source of motivation for dozens of entrepreneurs.

I learned from her story that being vulnerable and taking chances or risks can result in remarkable growth and success. It's about recognizing our anxieties and insecurities and finding the courage to overcome them. Magical things can occur when we open ourselves up to the outside world.

Let Shae's journey serve as a reminder that taking risks and being vulnerable can lead to extraordinary accomplishments.

Vulnerability is Not a Weakness!

Vulnerability is often viewed as a weakness, but it's actually a superpower that can help you grow and become stronger than ever before! When we embrace vulnerability, we unlock a world of exciting possibilities!

Here are the reasons why embracing vulnerability and taking risks is essential for personal growth and development:

- **Authenticity and Self-Expression:** Embracing vulnerability allows us to show our real selves and be authentic to our own selves. It helps us to express ourselves and the emotions that hold us back from being our true selves.

- **Emotional Growth and Resilience:** Vulnerability helps us to confront our fears and insecurities. It leads us to emotional growth and resilience.

- **Deeper Connections and Meaningful Relationships:** Vulnerability fosters deeper and more meaningful connections with other people. When we allow ourselves to be vulnerable, we inspire others to do the same and build a supportive community. This openness and authenticity can lead to incredibly meaningful relationships as we build trust, understanding, and empathy with each other.

- **Empowerment and Personal Freedom:** Embracing vulnerability and taking risks can lead us to take control of our lives and pursue our dreams and aspirations. It empowers us to overcome fear and self-doubt, enabling us to take bold steps and make meaningful choices. Embracing vulnerability also allows us to reach our full potential and live life on our own terms.

Overcoming the Fear of Failure

Failure is nothing but an opportunity for growth and self-development. I know that fear of failure can be paralyzing and can prevent us from taking risks and pursuing our dreams. But remember, failure isn't the end; it's actually the kick-start opportunity that helps you to achieve your goals and fulfill your dreams. Here are some of the techniques that will help you to overcome the fear of failure (Wooditch, 2019).

How I Overcame My Fear of Failure

Yes, I was also fearful of failure! I remember when I participated in an audition for the school play. I had always wanted to perform onstage, but I was afraid of failing. What if I stumbled on my lines? What if I failed to remember my prompts or dialogues? I was consumed by these thoughts, which made me question my abilities.

Then, I made the decision to confront my fear head-on. I prepared diligently, practicing my lines and rehearsing with a companion. Upon the arrival of the final audition, my heart dashed with anxiety, yet I took a deep breath and ventured onto the stage. I still can't believe I did that, lol!

During the tryout, I stuttered on a line and felt a flood of frenzy. But I didn't let it stop me; I just kept going. I embraced the chance of disappointment and told myself that it was part of enhancing my learning experience. I did the best that I could with it and left the audition with a feeling of achievement, no matter what the result.

Guess what, mate? I was not cast in the main role. However, that experience showed me important lessons and strengthened my confidence. I understood that disappointment doesn't characterize me; it's the manner by which I answer it that genuinely matters.

From that day forward, I embraced disappointment as a stepping stone to progress. I faced challenges, pursued my interests, and gained lessons from each misfortune. Each setback became an opportunity for self-improvement and growth. As I continued to push past my fear of failure, I also discovered my true potential and accomplished things I had previously considered impossible.

Thus, don't let the feeling of dread toward disappointment keep you down. Embrace it, learn from it, and allow it to drive you toward significance. Keep in mind the best way to genuinely fall flat is by never attempting.

With that, the following are some practices to help you be better at losing the fear of failure.

Adopt a Growth Mindset

Allow yourself to believe that failure doesn't define you or isn't a reflection of your abilities. It's an opportunity to grow and improve. See challenges as the stepping stones toward your final destination—your dreams!

Accept That Failure Is Normal and It Can Be a Good Thing

Understand the fact that life is not a bed of roses; failure is just a natural part of life. So, embrace it as a valuable lesson in disguise.

Pinpoint Exactly What You're Afraid Of

Identify the specific fears that hold you back from stepping out of your comfort zone and taking risks, then address and challenge those fears with confidence. I believe you, my dear. You can do this!

Give Yourself More Options

Look into different ways of reaching your goals, knowing that there is usually more than one right way. Embrace the freedom of your choice!

Answer Your "What If " Questions

Instead of thinking about the worst things that could happen, think about the good "what if" options. Look into the possible benefits and outcomes of taking risks.

Don't Just Visualize Success

Though visualizing success indeed helps, it's important to keep the journey in mind as well. Don't just solely focus on the outcome. Enjoy the steps you take and the knowledge you gain.

Focus On the Process, Not the Final Product

Stop focusing on the final product and start appreciating and learning from the process. Appreciate the development and learning that takes place as you go.

Remember, Failure Is Fleeting

Hey, remember, failure is just a temporary state. Don't let failure get you down! You'll bounce back in no time. Keep your chin up, and keep pushing yourself forward with resilience!

Finding Growth and Empowerment in First-Time Endeavors

Firsts hold a special place in everybody's life. Don't you just love "firsts?" They're like little badges of honor that remind us of all the amazing milestones we've achieved and the personal growth we've experienced.

Keep collecting those "firsts," and let's see how far we can go! Ah, the memories! Remember your first kiss? Or the first time you did anything intimate with a boy? How about your first dance or your first break-up? And who can forget their first time getting extremely drunk? Or that nerve-wracking first-time reading in front of the class?

And let's not forget the exhilarating feeling of driving for the first time! Ah, so many firsts to look back on with a smile.

When I got my first period, I was 11 and didn't know what it was. I cried because, at first, I thought I was dying, then I thought I was pregnant. I cried to my mom and told her I was pregnant and bleeding down there. She laughed and hugged me. I was so confused and scared. Then she said welcome to womanhood, and then she promptly called all the females in my family. Lol!

The first time I shaved my lady garden, down there. Ah, it was terrible! I actually went for the scissors first. Ouchie-wa-wa! Well, then I thought I could handle my dad's razor, but it turns out I'm not as skilled as I thought. I ended up with something that looked like it's been through a warzone. Who knew shaving could be so dangerous?

The first kiss! It was an awful experience. The boy I kissed was so stinky. I literally went and threw up after that. I don't even want to recall that kiss. But that's okay, at least I had a kiss. Lol.

These first-time experiences remind us how far we've come, but we still remember those silly moments. So, my queen, embrace those "firsts" and live an adventurous life!

Journal Prompts

Alright, time for some journal prompts to deepen your understanding of embracing first-time experiences:

- Think about something that makes you nervous or excited. Write down what you think and how you feel about it, and what you can do to feel confident about it.

- Think back to the first time you did something that didn't go as planned. What did you learn from the experience? How can you apply those lessons to future first-time endeavors?

- Recall an important first-time experience you're proud of. What lessons or ideas did you learn from that, and how can you use them in the future when you try something new?

Putting It All Together

Here are the major takeaways from this chapter:

- Look at new experiences as opportunities to grow and improve as a person.

- Embrace vulnerabilities as a catalyst for genuineness and connection with others.

- Failure is not the end but a chance to learn and get better.

- "Firsts" in life offer unique opportunities to grow and feel empowered.

- Reflect on the past to gain wisdom and apply it to future endeavors.

Key Takeaways

Well, we've explored the transformative power of embracing and learning from our "firsts" in life. By getting ready for new experiences, being vulnerable, overcoming the fear of failing, and finding growth and empowerment, we can open up a world of opportunities. Accept the magic of "firsts" and proudly step into the limitless possibilities that are waiting for you.

I'm happy for you that you've reached the end of this journey, and I want to reassure you that the lessons you've learned will help you have a better future.

Conclusion

Warriors, let's wrap up this epic self-help journey filled with beautiful memories and awe-inspiring anecdotes of some magical girls. Pat yourself on the back for the remarkable development you've undergone.

Think of yourself as the remarkable person you've become for a moment. We've delved into the depths of self-discovery, self-acceptance, and unleashing your inner awesomeness throughout this book.

Give me a virtual high five! It has been a roller coaster ride of development, empowerment, and accepting your individuality. Now is the time to bring everything home!

There is this one quote from Madonna that made me fix myself a lot. I myself felt so blue sometimes trying to be all perfect, you know. I am well aware of how we girls consider it an obligation to put up with worldly demands, right?

I laugh at myself. I don't take myself completely seriously. I think that's another quality that people have to hold on to... you have to laugh, especially at yourself. —Madonna

We strive to do so much! If the Queen of Pop herself does this, then we must follow her lead, mate! No cap!

It's all too easy to feel worthless over something that shouldn't even matter after a while because we are trying to be flawless, embarrassed over silly mistakes and self-sabotaging.

We should consider all of them as experiences, shaping us and helping us learn "How to live" this life. Madonna's quote reminded me how important it is to let go of these insecurities. It's okay not to "fit in."

We are meant to laugh at ourselves! It's the little moments that make us realize how full of life we girls are. I bet you will agree.

The most important takeaway: You are a formidable source of strength, potential, and endless possibilities.

Embrace the idea that you can create a life that lights up the sky, love every aspect of who you are, and embrace your true self.

I adore Rupi Kaur so much! Isn't she Amazing? I love her for her inspiring quotes, just like this one:

How you love yourself is how you teach others to love you. —Rupi Kaur

I mean, she very clearly said that if you can't love yourself, then how can you expect someone else to love you? Try to embrace yourself for every aspect of your personality. Trust me, your beauty lies in your confidence.

It's important to keep in mind this isn't the end, but rather a fresh start. It's your time to shine in the spotlight and conquer the game with the knowledge and inspiration you've gained. Take advantage of first-time experiences, achieve your objectives, and let your self-assurance sparkle like the brightest stars in the sky!

I want to leave you with a heartwarming success story. I once had a fellow student in tenth grade. She was exceptionally beautiful yet lacked so much confidence. Sarah used to be a shy teenager who once believed she lacked the skills necessary to make a difference. She embraced her distinctive voice, tapped into her inner strength, and courageously pursued her dreams with the advice she once read in a book.

Today, she's a pioneer, moving others with her immovable certainty and irresistible soul. Her story makes me believe how some experiences, words, and sayings transform you. Like honestly, she impresses me even today with her optimistic soul!

Now, it's your turn! All of this knowledge and inspiration needs to be put into practice, like, right away. Go out there and kill the game, embrace your uniqueness, and rock those first-time encounters with certainty.

You are absolutely incredible and can accomplish anything you set your mind to. Stay wild, become astounding, and continue to embrace your authentic self. Keep glowing and smile the widest! It looks so beautiful on you.

We are all in this together, so you are not alone on this journey. As we accept our flaws, laugh at ourselves, and radiate unshakable confidence, let's support and encourage one another.

I made it a priority to inject this book with fun, witty, and confidence-boosting elements that would make my teen girls feel as though they were conversing with their coolest BFF.

We are all human, and let's face it, we all make a lot of hilarious mistakes. Hopefully, you have learned to forgive yourself by now.

Repeat this to yourself: I am forgiving myself for everything, and I am ready to embrace my weaknesses and strengths to become more resilient!

I would be so appreciative if you could leave a review and share your thoughts on this self-help journey before we part ways. Your feedback will assist other amazing people in discovering this book and beginning their own transformative journey. Your feedback means everything to me as it assists in spreading positivity to other breathtaking young girls who are prepared to kill the game.

You are undergoing astonishing changes, and I am unable to keep myself calm. Please accept my sincere thanks for participating in this engaging experience with me.

Remember, you are destined to be amazing someday, and I put all my trust in you in every aspect of your life. Your light is needed everywhere. Now is the time to rock your teen years with unflinching self-assurance, infectious laughter, and a lot of girl power!

Go out there now and rule the world! The world is ready to be astonished by your uniqueness. Let's weave together a web of empowered individuals who encourage others to be completely themselves.

References

A Conscious Rethink. (2020). *15 truths to help you overcome your fear of being judged*. A Conscious Rethink. https://www.aconsciousrethink.com/12596/fe ar-of-being-judged/

Ackerman, C. E. (2018, August 6). *What is self-expression and how to Foster it? (20 Activities + Examples)*. PositivePsychology.com. https://positivepsychology.com/self-expression/

Adrian, T., Boyarchenko, N., & Giannone, D. (2019). Vulnerable Growth. *American Economic Review*, *109*(4), 1263–1289. https://doi.org/10.1257/aer.20161923

American Psychological Association. (2012). *Building your resilience*. Apa.org. https://www.apa.org/topics/resilience/buildin g-your-resilience

Anyiam, E. O. (2022). *Embracing Life*. WestBow Press.

Ashlin, P., & Kello, J. (2022). *5 actions of positive accountability*. iUniverse.

Athilakshmi, R., Ganesh, J., Maharishi Ranganathan, R., & Maya, R. (2015). Relationship between fear of negative evaluation and anxiety. *International Journal of Indian Psychology.* https://ijip.in/

Baker, M. C. (2018). *Living in a digital world: demystifying technology.* Createspace Interdependent Publishing Platform.

Branden, N. (1997). *Taking responsibility: self-reliance and the accountable life.* Simon & Schuster.

Carnegie, D., & Hadi, A. (2013). *How to win friends and influence people.* Pts Professional Pub.

Carson, S. H., & Langer, E. J. (2006). *Mindfulness and self-acceptance.* Journal of rational-emotive and cognitive-behavior therapy, 24(1), 29-43.

Cascio, C. N., O'Donnell, M. B., Tinney, F. J., Lieberman, M. D., Taylor, S. E., Strecher, V. J., & Falk, E. B. (2015). Self-affirmation activates brain systems associated with self-related processing and reward and is reinforced by future orientation. *Social Cognitive and Affective Neuroscience,* *11*(4), 621–629. https://doi.org/10.1093/scan/nsv136

Cherry, K. (2022). *How resilience helps with the coping of crisis.* Verywell Mind. https://www.verywellmind.com/what-is-resilience-2795059

Chubb, T. (2017). *The Power of Positive Energy.* Simon and Schuster.

Davis, S. (2021, September 13). *Self-advocacy: The basis of self-care.* CPTSDfoundation.org. https://cptsdfoundation.org/2021/09/13/self-advocacy-the-basis-of-self-care/

Engl, D. H. (2021). *Fear of judgement: why we are afraid of being judged.* Ness Labs. https://nesslabs.com/fear-of-judgement

Foad, B. S (1996). *Accountability.* Vantage Press.

Gordon, S. (2021). *EVerything your teen needs to know about setting boundaries.* Verywell Family. https://www.verywellfamily.com/boundaries-what-every-teen-needs-to-know-5119428#toc-how-to-set-boundaries

Guindon, M. H. (2002). Toward accountability in the use of the self-esteem construct. *Journal of Counseling & Development, 80*(2), 204–214. https://doi.org/10.1002/j.1556-6678.2002.tb00184.x

Hartney, E. (2022). *What is peer pressure?* Verywell Mind; Verywellmind. https://www.verywellmind.com/what-is-peer-pressure-22246

Hattie, J., & Timperley, H. (2007). The power of feedback. *Review of Educational Research, 77*(1), 81–112. https://doi.org/10.3102/003465430298487

Heckman, W. (2017). *6 common triggers of teen stress - the American institute of stress.* The American Institute of Stress. https://www.stress.org/6-common-triggers-of-teen-stress

Kabir, H. (n.d.). *Here's why accepting your imperfections can help you find meaning in life*. Happify.com. https://www.happify.com/hd/accepting-your-imperfections-can-help-you-find-meaning-in-life/

Kim, H. S., & Ko, D. (2007). *Culture and self-expression*. In C. Sedikides & S. Spencer (Eds.), Frontiers of social psychology: The self (pp. 325-342). New York, US: Psychology Press.

Kruzan, K. P., & Won, A. S. (2019). Embodied well-being through two media technologies: Virtual reality and social media. *New Media & Society*, *21*(8), 1734–1749. https://doi.org/10.1177/1461444819829873

Larson, S. (2009). *Embracing your freedom*. Moody Publishers.

Loureto, M. (2020, September 16). *How to embrace what makes you unique imagine sunsets*. Imagine Sunsets. https://imaginesunsets.com/2020/09/16/how-to-embrace-what-makes-you-unique/

MacInnes, D. L. (2006). Self-esteem and self-acceptance: an examination into their relationship and their effect on psychological health. *Journal of Psychiatric and Mental Health Nursing*, 13(5), 483-489.

Mahrer, B. (2019). *How accountability builds self-esteem.* HealthyPlace. https://www.healthyplace.com/blogs/buildings elfesteem/2019/5/how-accountability-builds-self-esteem

Mitchell, C. B., & Carson, D. A. (2021). *How do we live in a digital world?* Lexham Press.

Pugle, M. (2021). *What is stress and how can I recognize it?* Verywell Health. https://www.verywellhealth.com/what-is-stress-5190229

Pugle, M. (2022, September 13). *Peer pressure: Types, examples, tips for teens and adults.* Verywell Health. https://www.verywellhealth.com/peer-pressure-in-teen-and-adult-life-5323858

Rekhi, S. (n.d.). *SElf-acceptance: Definition, quotes, & how to practice it.* The Berkeley Well-Being Institute. https://www.berkeleywellbeing.com/self-acceptance.html

Schroth, S. (2022). *Positive words, positive vibes.* Dorrance Publishing.

Scott, E. (2022, June 10). *How to handle stressful situations.* Verywell Mind. https://www.verywellmind.com/how-to-adapt-to-a-stressful-situation-3144674#toc-have-the-right-attitude

Self-acceptance and happiness. In The strength of self-acceptance (pp. 121-137). Springer, New York, NY.

Self acceptance quotes (500 quotes). (n.d.). Www.goodreads.com. https://www.goodreads.com/quotes/tag/self-acceptance

Singh, A. (2021). *HOw to stop your fear of being judged hold you back.* Calm Sage - Your Guide to Mental and Emotional Well-Being. https://www.calmsage.com/how-to-stop-your-fear-of-being-judged/

Singh, R. (2022, January 2). *EXpressing yourself: A guide to self-expression | MantraCare.* Mantra Care. https://mantracare.org/therapy/what-is/expressing-yourself/

Smith, G. (2013). *Positive vibes.* Hay House, Inc.

Spearman, J., & Harrison, L. (2010). *Real role models.* University of Texas Press.

Stone, H., & Stone, S. (2011). *Embracing our selves.* New World Library.

Szentagotai, A., & David, D. (2013). *Self-acceptance and happiness.* In The strength of self-acceptance (pp. 121-137). Springer, New York, NY.

Teodoro, A. (2017). *The power of positive energy : powerful thinking, powerful life : 9 powerful ways for self-improvement, increasing self-esteem, & gaining positive energy, motivation, forgiveness, happiness & peace of mind.* Createspace Independent Publishing Platform.

Tiggemann, M., & Anderberg, I. (2019). *Social media is not real: The effect of "Instagram vs reality" images on women's social comparison and body image.* New Media & Society, 22(12), 2183–2199. https://doi.org/10.1177/1461444819888720

Wendy, L. (2021, March 21). *The emotional benefits of feeling unique | Psychology Today.* https://www.psychologytoday.com/us/blog/why-bad-looks-good/202103/the-emotional-benefits-feeling-unique

Wooditch, B. (2019). *Fail more: embrace, learn, and adapt to failure as a way to success.* McGraw-Hill Education.

Yaribeygi, H., Panahi, Y., Sahraei, H., Johnston, T. P., & Sahebkar, A. (2017). *The impact of stress on body function: A review. EXCLI Journal, 16(1), 1057–1072.* https://doi.org/10.17179/excli2017-480